Portable feasts

Portable feasts

Clare Ferguson

Photography by **Jeremy Hopley**

jacqui
small

Dedication

To my parents, whose pleasure in decent food, good cooking, conviviality and picnicking set me up for life, and to my sisters, Alison and Patricia, who, like me, continue these traditions, with love and laughter, to this very day.

I also thank my husband, Ian, for his love and encouragement.

Notes:
• All measures are level unless otherwise stated.
• Fresh herbs should be used unless otherwise stated. If substituting dried herbs use a half or a quarter the amount. Better still, substitute another fresh herb.
• Dishes containing uncooked or partly cooked eggs should not be served to young children, or to anyone who is sick, elderly or pregnant.
• Raw milk cheeses, similarly, should not be served to young children, or to anyone who is sick, elderly or pregnant.
• Rare-cooked meats should not be served to anyone who is pregnant.

Publisher Jacqui Small
Editor Madeline Weston
Designer Robin Rout
Additional photography Robin Rout
Food stylist Clare Ferguson
Assistant food stylist Bethany Heald
Stylist Wei Tang
Production Geoff Barlow

First published in 2002 by Jacqui Small, an imprint of Aurum Press Ltd, 25 Bedford Avenue, London WC1B 3AT

Text copyright © Clare Ferguson 2001

Photography, design and layout copyright © Jacqui Small 2001

The right of Clare Ferguson to be identified as the Author of this Work has been asserted by her in accordance with the Copyright, Designs and Patents Act 1988.

A catalogue record for this book is available from the British Library.

ISBN 1 90322 1110

Printed and bound in China

Contents

Some of my fondest childhood memories involve food eaten out of doors or in unorthodox situations. As a busy adult such activities still delight me. After a long day's work or a complicated week I am often to be found coaxing my husband, neighbours and friends into joining me for an open-air feast in the local park.

Friends may be urged to provide some chilled wine or beers or spring water. We two will pillage the fridge and the pantry: snatch olives, olive oil, pepper and salt grinders, lemons, cold fish pâté and a crisp cucumber or lettuce. Along will come a packet of nougat or amaretti biscuits. Packed into our baskets will be plates, cutlery, glasses, a corkscrew and paper napkins. In seconds we are off.

En route we will pick up a freshly cooked rôtisserie chicken, foil-wrapped, and some crusty flutes or baguettes. If the melons or grapes look good and smell scented we'll grab some of these, too.

When we all meet up at the park and select our favourite bench in a niche in the mossy walls, we sit back, survey the flowers and breathe a long sigh. Some of the stresses and strains of our lives unravel. Corks fly. Bottles pop. Glasses clink. The joy of spending precious time among friends, feasting, is something I find both restorative and fascinating.

We pass the bread, pull off warm chicken using our fingers and sip. We are at peace. Outbreaks of laughter happen easily. We exchange ideas, gossip, commiserate, relax.

Portable Feasts celebrates informality and fun: these elevate casual eating to an art. Care to join me? This book is an invitation to conviviality.

Choose ideas from the hundred and more here: a collection of 'little feasts', sumptuous appetisers and hors d'oeuvre, with drinks to match. Or select some sandwiches, pastries and cakes for an outdoor 'tea'. Maybe you'd prefer some main dishes served warm straight from their containers or some barbecue bounty cooked right on the spot? On the following pages you will find all these, along with appealing sweet feasts which are also portable: fresh fruity desserts, baking and frivolous cookies.

Food should be inspirational but easy. With this in mind, many of the chosen ideas are intriguing, multicultural dishes. Included are many fascinating spicy dressings, seasonings, marinades, ethnic wraps and salads; interesting pâtés, dips and spreads as well as magnificent main course dishes. There are kebabs, pasta dishes and brownies; cocktails, old-fashioned cordials and tisanes.

Sand in the sandwiches, slugs in the salad? These are nobody's idea of fun. Advice about how to prepare, pack and present these delicacies is built into the book's structure along with countless full-page colour

photographs. Often taken on site, these pictures enliven each situation. Food must arrive at its destination fresh, safe and undamaged. Appropriate containers and serving tools are also considered, and much of the pleasure of eating out of doors comes from showing off your feast to advantage. This is a talent you can easily acquire. Follow the many professional tips we have included in this book and any portable feast you make will be a wild success.

Basic common sense helps make meals on the move more enjoyable, less fraught with mishaps. Butter is no use if it is a liquid pool on the bottom of the container; strawberry jam tastes best from an unbroken pot, wine is frustrating when you've forgotten your corkscrew or the glasses.

It is easy to develop an instinct for organisation and a spirit for innovation. *Portable Feasts* celebrates both these concepts along with a belief in delicious, fresh food, handsomely served. But where? The venue can be anywhere you choose. Location is up to you.

A leisurely trip to the ball game or to a school sports day will be more memorable if you've managed to take a few delicious snacks and drinks for having en route. *Portable Feasts* provides meals, snacks and drinks for those on the move: romantic suppers for couples; children's parties under the trees, fun for everyone. The recipes were developed to complement and offset one another, resulting in scores of different menu combinations to suit many different occasions.

When planning your meal consider pairing up recipes that can be prepared in advance with others that can be done on the spot: sautéed, barbecued or bonfire-cooked dishes. Combine, with these, some good quality delicatessen food, fresh produce, breads, cheeses, beers, wines and fruit juices. Not only does this make the planning simpler but it also makes each meal a unique event. Local specialities such as fresh seafood, wild mushrooms and herbs, orchard fruits growing on the trees, are factors which can become celebrations in their own right.

Finally, participation on the part of your fellow eaters can make this mode of entertaining much more democratic, far more fun. Children may surprise you: those who would not dream of peeling the potatoes at home may prove expert at wraps and kebabs. Partners who profess to be novices at the kitchen sink often blossom into people precise at packing hampers; brilliant at building a barbecue, gifted at making a gin fizz.

For them, and for you, this book is a celebration of the possible; and how you can make epicures of everyone. Enjoy your own portable feasts, wherever they may be.

Essential kit

To keep food or drink in a perfect state of freshness, hotness or coldness, needs some ingenuity and wit, but not necessarily expense. Ordinary household items such as cool boxes, vacuum flasks and jugs, screw-top jars and bottles, snap-top plastic containers, clip-top jars can be utilised. Plastic or metal buckets, bowls or bags; metal or plastic bottle carriers as well as wooden hampers, wickerwork or metal boxes can all be pressed into service. Metal cutlery, chopsticks, toughened glasses, durable crockery will often fit the bill. But there is also, now, a superb selection of specially designed kit made from colourful, unbreakable plastic, melamine, metal and coated paper, softwoods, woven fibres and shatterproof glass. There are also disposables: pretty tumblers, plates, cups, cutlery, napkins, bottleholders and bowls. On-site cooking needs particular equipment: camping gas cookers, portable cooking rings, fuelled by a gas cartridge, and wind-proof stoves are possibilities. Go to camping and leisure stores. Many barbecues exist: some tiny, disposable and cheap, others robust, large char-broilers, gas fired, often with wheels. Outdoor fires and pit cooking are fun for the more adventurous – but do follow our safety instructions – and take appropriate kindling, aromatic woods and charcoal, and scented herbs for added savour. Don't forget the corkscrew and the cushions!

A folding plastic carrying box is ideal for holding all your food containers as well as plastic tumblers and vacuum flasks.

A strongly woven nylon bag with handles to carry your picnic. The plastic boxes all have snap-top lids to keep food fresh.

A neatly divided lunch box keeps different foods separate; stacking plastic tumblers are both safe and space saving.

The old-fashioned style of ginger beer bottle keeps your fizzy and still drinks secure; carry your bottles in an ice bucket.

Your ice bucket can be converted into a washing-up bowl when the feasting is over. Take a brush along with you.

Stainless steel cutlery may be heavier but it is a pleasure to use. Bowls and buckets are useful for salads and ice. –

This camping stove, using methylated spirit for fuel, cleverly packs away to make it easy to carry. See right.

Unpacked, the stove contains a kettle, 3 pans, and a frying pan. Lightweight, it is useful for cooking for small numbers.

A windproof stove burning camping gas and a lightweight kettle mean you can have a cup of tea literally anywhere!

Vacuum flasks come in many sizes and styles: stainless steel, plastic and toughened glass or ceramic are all practical.

This small portable barbecue is made of galvanised metal and has its own grill rack. It has a drawer to remove the ash.

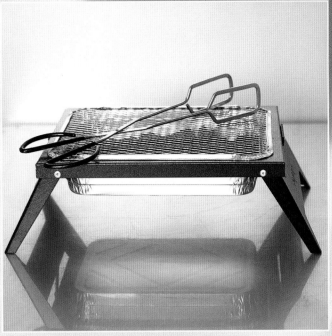

Set your disposable barbecue tray in this folding metal holder, and have the best of both worlds, with no mess to clear up.

The traditional cast-iron French barbecue rack can be placed directly over the charcoal. Start your fire in a safe place!

This large galvanised metal barbecue can be found in Greek shops. The rack folds back to cook kebabs over the coals.

Some useful items include a penknife, can opener, tongs, oyster knife, corkscrew, camping plates and wooden spoons.

Galvanised metal storage boxes with handles could carry camping storage containers and stainless mixing bowls.

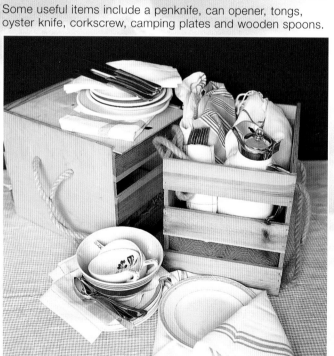

Wooden carrying hampers are stylish and practical with sliding lids and rope handles. Wrap your crockery in napkins.

Durable melamine picnic crockery and attractive wooden cutlery are easily transported in a tough plastic shopping bag.

A wire trug basket makes the ideal carrier for toughened glasses, each wrapped in a pretty table napkin.

A stool or a table, according to your needs. This lightweight camping stool can double up as either and is easy to carry.

Rugs, throws and cushions are an essential. Sit on them, eat off them, and lie back and rest after the feast is over.

Picnicking at dusk? A pressure lamp and lanterns will light your feast. Citronella candles will keep mosquitoes at bay.

Small feasts

Little mouthfuls of delicious, tasty, savoury nibbles can do more than merely awaken the appetite: they can enliven the whole meal. Sometimes one item alone is enough for a splendid little feast. Follow it by a crisp or juicy piece of fresh fruit, add a glass of sparkling water, some juice, wine or beer and suddenly you've made a perfectly balanced small feast.

Alternatively combine several snack items from this chapter for an *al fresco* party or use one recipe in the time-honoured way, as the first of several courses. Many choices from soups to nuts to rillettes are included here: enjoy yourself selecting and combining them to suit your own style, your particular occasion.

Radishes, French Style *page 18*

Tapénade *page 20*

Green Pea & Prosciutto Soup *page 32*

The recipes in this first chapter are for appetite arousing: delicious snacks and small savoury items or soups. These can be eaten or drunk on their own, grouped together informally as a snack meal, or teamed up with other dishes from the following chapters to make more complex menus. The format is fluid: any number of marvellous menus of any style can be built up from a creative selection of these recipes with your own accompaniments.

When combining recipes do not be too ambitious. Two or three new ideas at the most, combined with some ready-prepared, bought items such as bread, cheese, fruit and some good thing to drink, would seem a realistic aim.

On the other hand, combining a beautiful bunch of fresh radishes with butter and salt may be an entirely novel concept. It is utterly delectable. Clean, fresh, crisp and still-cold radishes in a leafy bunch; some perfect butter, flaky salt: such choices not only make sense but add pleasure and give style to the most minimal of meals.

Do not underestimate the importance of contrast: sophisticated foods with earthy ones; hot with cold; rich with plain; spicy with mild; let colours remain vivid: leave good-looking produce whole whenever possible, not only because it looks more lovely, but because it is likely to retain more of its original food value as well. And it saves time and effort.

Be creative: smoked trout pâté and matzoh crackers may work wonderfully with borscht or black bean soup, served in bowls you can sip from. Salted almonds followed by beignets with a flask of hot pea soup may be just the thing on a cool day in spring – all you need.

Palmiers, spiced cheese and green salad may seem enough for a mini-feast. Blini and taramasalata, without the 'saviar' (salmon caviar being sophisticated fare), may be best eaten utterly on their own.

Suit your drinks to your circumstances: drivers must be offered non-alcoholic alternatives. Anyway there are wonderful soft drinks, and herb- and fruit-based drinks you can offer, as well as alcohol-free cocktails of great charm and freshness. The alternative is to buy some still or sparkling spring water en route, some oranges, limes or a grapefruit and a bag of ice cubes. This way you make fabulous fresh drinks to order, on the spot. (But be sure to have packed unbreakable glasses or else carry ordinary goblets in a wire tray or wrap up each glass in a cloth napkin.)

Tapénade with soft-boiled eggs and baguette: some crisp, salad leaves followed by new potatoes with blue cheese and a glass or two of Pernod or Ricard, topped up 1 part to 5 with iced water. This is a gallic feast fit for a dauphin. Yet it consists of little things, easily organised.

Mini game burgers then some tagliatelle with truffle butter, a bunch or two of black grapes or some dried muscat raisins, teamed with a formidable Côtes du Rhône or a Shiraz and you'll feel that autumn's bounty is a celebration in itself.

Imagination, delectable recipe ideas, decent bread, appropriate wine, seasonal fruits and regional produce, and you have every chance of becoming a portable feast *aficionado*. Whether you take your little feast upstairs to bed or out into the park; off to the beach or aboard a boat: soon you'll discover that pleasure is a state of mind.

So relax, and *bon appétit* – use these ideas to devise your very own, easy style of entertaining.

Parmesan & Poppy Seed Palmiers

These pretty, curlicued pastries are a savoury version of the classic sweet ones. Paradoxically, they taste good dusted with icing sugar at serving time. To carry them, pack them into a napkin-lined box or shallow basket.

Makes 32–36

To buy/find

750g bought puff pastry in the block (or pre-rolled)

4 tablespoons Dijon mustard

4 tablespoons blue poppy seeds

4 tablespoons grated Parmesan cheese (from the block)

2 tablespoons icing sugar

To prepare/cook Roll out or unfold the chilled pastry into a rectangle about 20 x 70cm, and about 3mm thick. Trim the edges. Spread the pastry first with mustard, then poppy seeds, then cheese. Starting from both short sides, roll each in tightly towards the centre so that they meet in a double roll with a 'ram's horn' appearance. Turn the double roll over so that the flat side is up. Using a long, serrated knife and pressing firmly, slice down, crosswise, to give 32–36 slim palmiers. Water spray, or wet by hand, 4 or more baking sheets and lay the palmiers on them, allowing space between each. Chill for 1 hour. Bake 2 sheets at a time in an oven preheated to 230°C for 6–7 minutes or until they start to caramelise underneath. With a fish slice, carefully turn each palmier over. Bake again for a further 4–5 minutes or until crispy and caramelised. Repeat with the remaining palmiers until they are all cooked. Cool completely on wire racks. Store in an airtight container for up to 7 days.

To present Dust them lightly with icing sugar, using a fine sieve, at serving time.

Radishes, French Style

French gourmets (and gourmands!) treat radishes with a respect they are rarely accorded in other countries. The crunch of radish, cold and clean, a dot of butter, a tingle of sea salt flakes – and the meal is under way. Select beautiful radish specimens: crimson or pink and white, in fat bunches, leaves intact. Choose lovely butter, maybe French *Echiré* (which comes, conveniently, in tiny wooden pails containing 250g) and Maldon sea salt flakes or the French equivalent. Kosher salt would do.

Serves 4

To buy/find

2–3 bunches fresh, crisp radishes with leaves

unsalted or lightly salted butter, e.g. *Echiré*

50g Maldon sea salt flakes, *sel du mer* or kosher salt

To present Have the washed, chilled radishes in a cloth-lined basket or box with the (room temperature) butter still in its pail, if possible, and a lidded small pot of salt. Encourage your companions to break off a radish, dunk in butter, dip in salt, eat.

Note:

Some Poilâne or other good sourdough bread might be a nice accompaniment.

Spiced Cheese

with Crudités

This is based on the famous dish of Liptauer: a soft, fresh mild but spreadable cheese popular in Hungary and Austria, traditionally served surrounded by heaps of salt, paprika, mustard, butter, chives and caraway seeds. In this version they are all stirred in. Try this spread with crisp, seasonal vegetables cut into strips, sticks or rings: it is hugely adaptable. Chill well before taking out of doors, especially if on active pursuits.

Makes about 450g, Serves 8

To buy/find

300g curd cheese, cream cheese or low fat soft cheese

50g salted butter

2 tablespoons hot mustard powder

2 teaspoons hot red paprika

2 tablespoons freshly grated horseradish (optional)

2 tablespoons chopped fresh chives

1/2 teaspoon salt

2 tablespoons caraway seeds

Crudités:

Choose from cucumber, peppers, spring onions, onion rings, button mushrooms, baby vine tomatoes, carrot and perhaps breadsticks, crispbreads and crackers.

To prepare/make Cream the cheese and butter together until well blended, and stir in all the remaining ingredients. Pack in individual snap-top boxes, cartons or bowls. Put the selection of crudités in a second, but similar container, ideally rigid, so they stay undamaged in transit.

Salted Almonds

These treats, learned from a Greek cook, are blissfully simple but very appealing for nibbling. Once made and completely cold, they'll keep for ages in an airtight jar. And although they look dark and strange, they have a satisfying crunch and taste superb at any portable feast. A great snack.

Makes about 500g

To buy/find

25g citric acid crystals (from pharmacy or specialist deli)

75ml hand-hot water

500g shelled, unblanched almonds

25g table salt

To prepare/cook Toss the citric acid crystals into the water. Stir to dissolve. Spread out the almonds in 2 large flat ovenproof trays or dishes, such as roasting pans. Pour the citric acid water over the almonds and leave until well absorbed: about 20 minutes. Drain off excess liquid. Sprinkle the salt over and turn the almonds in it so that they are coated. Bake the almonds, uncovered, in an oven preheated to 180°C, towards the top, for 35–40 minutes, stirring twice. Cool on the trays. Once the nuts are completely cold, scoop them up, shaking off the excess salt, and pack into airtight jars. They keep for weeks. To transport, take handfuls from the jar and pack into a twist of foil or waxed paper, secured with some string.

To present Undo and let people help themselves.

Note:

If citric acid proves unobtainable, use the equivalent volume of freshly-squeezed lemon juice – though the acidity level is not quite as intense.

Tapénade with Eggs & Baguette

Proper, Provençale tapénade is a revelation: the pungent flavours sing out at you and it looks dark, glossy and handsome. Surround it with brilliantly yellow-yolked soft-boiled eggs and some sliced or torn crisp baguette and you have a feast for eyes, nose and palate. But it is essential to ensure all your ingredients are superb. This generous tapénade recipe makes enough for 4 meals: it keeps well in the refrigerator for weeks, though its accompaniments must always be fresh on the day.

Makes about 675g tapénade, Serves 16
Presentation serves 4

To buy/find

500g dry-cured (ideally French) salted black olives

185g canned tuna, olive oil packed

80g canned or salted anchovies, drained and chopped

75g pickled or salted capers

5–6 garlic cloves, crushed

2 teaspoons fresh thyme leaves or 1/2 teaspoon dried

30ml extra virgin olive oil

15–30ml cognac or brandy

4 free-range, organic eggs

1 baguette loaf

To prepare/cook Pit the olives. (Do not even consider using the pre-pitted, water-packed, chemically-dyed type: they are a travesty.) Put the olive flesh, the tuna, flaked, and its oil, the anchovies and capers (well rinsed in warm water, twice) and the garlic and thyme into a large mortar or food-processor. Pound using a pestle, or process, in brief bursts, in the food-processor, to a rough black paste. Now drizzle in the olive oil, continuing to pound or process, making the paste glossier still. Finally stir in the cognac or brandy. Spoon into a large lidded pot or bowl. Refrigerate. To soft-boil the eggs: allow them to come to room temperature, cover them with hand-hot water, bring to the boil and simmer for 4–5 minutes. Cool under running cold water. Scoop about 50g tapénade per person into the mortar or a pot for transporting. Remove the eggshells and pack the eggs separately.

To present When at the site, halve the eggs crosswise. Slice or tear some baguette. Surround the tapénade with egg halves and bread. Encourage diners to dip the egg into the tapénade and eat, alternating egg with a bite of baguette.

Hummus

This Middle Eastern dip and spread, which, strictly, should be called *hummus bi tahini*, since it contains tahini (not all versions of hummus do) is delicious when made at home, even if you use canned chickpeas.

Makes about 700g

To buy/find

500g freshly cooked or canned chickpeas (about 225g, if cooked from dry)

3 tablespoons tahini (toasted sesame seed paste)

4 tablespoons freshly squeezed lemon juice

4 garlic cloves, crushed

3/4 teaspoon salt

125ml extra virgin olive oil

To serve:

Paprika, flatleaf parsley, optional flatbreads

To prepare/cook Drain the cooked chickpeas but reserve some of the liquid. Put the chickpeas into a food processor with the tahini, juice, garlic and salt. Process in several long bursts to a gritty paste. With the machine running, drizzle in 110ml of the olive oil through the feed tube until you have a thick, rich, creamy purée. Do not over-process – a little roughness can still taste good. If it seems too dense, or intense, process again, in brief bursts, adding 6–8 tablespoons of cooking liquid, until it is the texture you like. Serve the hummus cool, straight away, or chill it if it is to be used at a later time: it keeps well, in the refrigerator, for up to 1 week.

To present Serve with the reserved olive oil drizzled over the hummus in its bowl, a pinch of paprika and some parsley sprigs, adding warmed torn flatbreads as needed.

Casa Rosita's Guacamole

Many friends have mentioned Rosita's famous restaurant in New York to me; I long to visit it soon. Here is my guacamole, based upon Rosita's version. It is superb.

Makes 400g or 6–8 servings

To buy/find

1 medium white, or 1 small Spanish, onion, chopped

150g bunch fresh coriander leaves

2 teaspoons sea salt or kosher salt

4 garlic cloves, crushed

4 ripe Hass avocados

2 limes, halved, to garnish (optional)

2 green and 1 red chilli, sliced

1/2 teaspoon dried oregano (optional)

2 plum tomatoes, cut in 1cm cubes

To serve:

Tostaditas, tortilla crisps, warmed tortillas, torn

To prepare/make Using a big *molcahete* (Mexican mortar) or big mortar and pestle (or, less satisfactorily, a food-processor), combine the onion, coriander, salt and garlic and pound and mash, or process in brief bursts, to a green aromatic paste. Now scoop in the avocado flesh. Add a squeeze of fresh lime, if you like (Rosita does not do this) and the green chillies. Stir, pound, mix or process briefly again. Crumble the oregano on top, if using. (Again, Rosita does not). Decorate with a tumble of red jewel-like tomato cubes and red chillies.

To present Serve in the *molcahete* or mortar or a bowl surrounded by the lime halves and the tostaditas, crisps and torn tortilla bits.

Salsa

Salsa cruda, generally of Mexican origin, means an uncooked sauce made from finely chopped savoury ingredients with some acidity from citrus juice or vinegar. Some salsas contain oil; this one does not. It tastes fresh and lively. Hand chopped – not machine processed – salsas taste best.

Makes about 400ml

To buy/find

I red onion, finely chopped

3 plum or vine tomatoes, finely cubed

2 hot fresh red or green chillies, deseeded, deveined and chopped

juice of 2 limes or 1 lemon (5–6 tablespoons)

2 tablespoons stock or water

sea salt flakes and crushed allspice, to taste

1 handful fresh coriander, mint, parsley, chives or thyme, or a mix, chopped

To prepare/make Combine the ingredients in a non-reactive bowl, stirring. Taste, adjust seasonings as needed. Use the same day.

To present Serve in small or large bowls.

Variations

Substitute 3 spring onions for the red onion.

Substitute blanched, dehusked tomatillos, or green tomatoes, for the red tomatoes.

Add 1 teaspoon finely shredded fresh root ginger and black pepper instead of allspice and use all coriander, for an Asian-style salsa.

Add 3–4 tablespoons of extra virgin olive oil for a richer effect.

Blini

with Taramasalata & 'Saviar'

Blini are yeast-risen pancakes, Russian in origin. Traditionally made of buckwheat, they are, these days, often made with part wheat flour, part buckwheat flour, or even 100% wheat flour. This recipe makes 48 blini, so freeze what you don't need for another occasion. Taramasalata, a Greek classic, should be made using pressed, salted cod's roe from a Greek deli. Substitute some salted, smoked cod's roe in the piece from a good fishmonger if none can be found: not authentic but good, even so. Time at a premium? Purchase ready-made blini, ready-made taramasalata and add the salmon 'caviar' (also known as 'saviar' or keta) as a garnish.

Makes 48
Allow 3–4 blini, 25g taramasalata and 1 large teaspoon 'saviar' per person for an appetiser; double this for a main course

To buy/find

Blini:

200g strong white bread flour

50g buckwheat flour

1 teaspoon or 1/2 sachet micronised, easyblend yeast

1 teaspoon sea salt flakes

275ml milk, warmed to blood heat

150ml soured cream

2 eggs, separated

6 tablespoons butter or olive oil, for cooking

Taramasalata:

4 tablespoons *tarama*: salted, pressed, cod's roe, or 100g salted, smoked cod's roe, skinned, chopped

2 thick slices white bread, wetted and squeezed dry

2 garlic cloves, crushed

1 lemon

250ml extra virgin olive oil

3–4 tablespoons boiling water

handful fresh parsley, chopped

100g pot 'saviar' (salmon 'caviar')

To prepare/cook blinis Sift together the flours, yeast and salt in a large heatproof bowl. Add the warmed milk, the soured cream and the egg yolks, and lightly beat together to make a thick batter. Cover using a large plastic bag. Set on a rack over hand-hot water, not touching the bowl, or in another warm place. Leave for 40–50 minutes or until risen. Now whisk the egg whites to a stiff foam and fold in carefully. Preheat a large griddle, hot plate, non-stick or cast iron frying pan. Add 1 tablespoon butter or olive oil. Spoon 8 dessert-spoonfuls of batter, from the tip of the spoon, to make small pancakes. Once the batter meets the hot surface it sets and bubbles will soon show on the uncooked upper surface. When this happens turn them over and cook again, briefly, until golden on the second side. Test one: it should be cooked right through. Cook the remaining batter in batches in more hot butter or olive oil. Cool on wire racks. Pack the cooled blini, in stacks, in a cloth- or napkin-lined little basket or box for transporting.

To prepare taramasalata Put the *tarama* or smoked cod's roe into a food-processor with the wet, crumbled bread, the garlic and juice of half the lemon. Process briefly until mixed. Now, with the machine running, drizzle in the oil, in a thin, fine stream until the mixture stiffens into a dense paste. Scrape down the sides as necessary. Now drizzle in 3–4 tablespoons of boiling water (or more as needed) with the machine running, to lighten the texture. Throw in the parsley and stop the machine. Pack the finished taramasalata into a medium-sized china or toughened glass jar or pot with a lid. If necessary wrap in plastic wrap or a wet cloth for transporting.

To present Set out the blini, opened taramasalata and the opened 'saviar' with the remaining lemon half. Have small knives or spoons ready for scooping and spreading.

Mini Game Burgers

with Bacon

Delicious, gamey meat patties with juniper and Armagnac to accentuate the autumnal tastes. In France these are called *gaillettes* or *caillettes*, depending on the region and dialect. They are just the thing for a sporty day out.

Makes 800g, 16 burgers
Allow 2 burgers per serving as an appetiser

To buy/find

185g boneless, skinless duck, boar or pheasant, in 1cm cubes

250g smoked streaky bacon

4 tablespoons Armagnac

6 tablespoons chopped fresh herbs e.g. parsley, rosemary, thyme or oregano

1 small onion, finely chopped

salt and freshly ground black pepper

350g minced beef or veal

50g fresh breadcrumbs

2 teaspoons juniper berries, crushed

1 egg, beaten

2 tablespoons extra virgin olive oil

To prepare/cook Put the diced game into a non-reactive bowl. Reserve half the bacon; finely scissor-chop or mince the rest, and add to the bowl. Add the Armagnac and the herbs, onion and the seasonings. Marinate for 20 minutes, or several hours in the refrigerator, then stir in the minced meat, breadcrumbs, crushed juniper berries and the egg. Mix well, kneading with clean hands to make a dense meat paste. Stretch each reserved bacon slice using a knife blade and halve lengthwise. Divide the meat into 16 equal portions. Squeeze each portion tightly into a ball then flatten into a burger about 5cm across. Wrap a bacon slice around the outer circumference. Hold it in place with a wooden cocktail stick. Repeat until all are prepared. Heat the oil in a large heavy-based or non-stick frying pan. Add the burgers and sauté over medium-high heat for 3–4 minutes on the first side, and 2–3 minutes on the second. The burgers should be slightly rosy inside, but if you prefer, cook them longer until *à point* (to your liking). Remove the cocktail sticks.

To present Serve hot, warm or cold (but not chilled) with spring onions or salad leaves of the season. Eat using the fingers or with a knife and fork.

Pork Rillettes

with Endive and Rolls

Lean they are not, but rillettes, to my mind, are one of the glories of *cuisine bourgeoise*. Good delis and speciality grocers may stock rillettes in glass pots. Buy some: they are a great larder standby. But make your own once, and you'll be converted. Make them at least one day ahead: they keep, refrigerated and well sealed, for weeks. If you wish, substitute up to a third of the pork with pickled belly pork in place of fresh, or with duck, goose, rabbit or hare.

Makes about 800g, Serves 8

To buy/find

1.5kg belly pork, including rind

4 garlic cloves

1/2 nutmeg, grated (1 teaspoon grated nutmeg)

1–2 tablespoons black peppercorns, coarsely crushed

1 1/2–2 tablespoons sea salt flakes or kosher salt

75g bunch parsley stalks, tied with string

1 sprig (3–4 leaves) fresh bay, bruised

50g fresh thyme sprigs, plus extra to garnish

To serve:

8 crusty bread rolls

1 head chicory

To prepare/cook Remove the pork rind in one piece and any bones and cartilage, and set aside. Now chop the meat into 2.5cm chunks. Put the rind, fat side down, in the base of a flameproof casserole. Add the meat, bones, cartilage and remaining ingredients. Pour in 100ml of cold water; cover tightly. Bring the pan contents to a simmer, check, cover tightly again and turn to the lowest possible heat, or put into a low oven preheated to 130°C. Cook, undisturbed, for about 3 hours until the meat and fat disintegrate. Do not let the pan boil dry: add a few tablespoons of water, as needed, now and then to prevent any signs of frying. Remove casserole from the heat. Pour pan contents into a sieve over a bowl. Discard rind, bones, cartilage, any other debris such as bay leaves and stems. Using clean fingers or two forks, tease apart and shred the solids. Put in a clean bowl. Add enough of the strained fat to create a creamy paste. Smooth the mixture into one large or several small jars or pots. Drizzle over extra fat, thinly, to seal. Push reserved thyme sprigs into the fat to garnish. Once the rillettes are completely cold, refrigerate. Add lids or tops after several hours of chilling. Take the pots to your site.

To present Let people help themselves: scoop the rillettes into each split roll to make a thick layer and push in some chicory leaves. (If the rolls are made ahead, wrap them in waxed paper.)

Salmon-Rice Beignets

in Mini-Romaine Leaves

Smoked salmon, cooked rice, seasonings and eggs combine to make 'beignets', golden and puffy, to eat in the fingers, and easy to transport in back-pack or pannier bag. They are good cool rather than chilled. Fold each in little leaves before eating. *Shichimi togarashi* is a kind of Japanese seven-spice mix: go to an Asian deli for this and for *wasabi* powder, an alternative.

Makes 24, Serves 8

To buy/find

125g smoked salmon, scissor-chopped

125g cooked white or brown long grain rice or wild rice

6 spring onions, chopped

2 teaspoons *shichimi togarashi* seasoning or
1/2 teaspoon *wasabi* powder

3 tablespoons tomato juice

2 eggs, separated

sea salt and freshly ground black pepper

4 tablespoons extra virgin olive oil

4 heads mini-romaine (Little Gem) lettuces

2 limes, quartered

To prepare/cook Combine the smoked salmon, rice, spring onions, seasoning, tomato juice and egg yolks in a bowl, stirring with a fork. Do not mash. In a small separate high-sided bowl whisk the egg whites with a pinch of the salt to a stiff foam. Fold this into the salmon-rice mixture with about 1 teaspoon of salt, and pepper to taste. Heat 1 tablespoon of the oil in a non-stick or heavy-based frying pan. Spoon in 6 small portions (about a tablespoon each) of mixture. Reduce the heat to low. Cook until golden and crusty, 1 1/2–2 minutes on each side. Test one: it must be cooked right through. Repeat with more oil until you have finished the mixture (total of 4 batches). Cool the beignets to room temperature. Chill them if they are to travel far. Pack the washed, whole lettuces separately, wrapped in wet kitchen paper with some ice cubes. Enclose in a plastic clip-top bag or box. Pack the cool beignets in another box.

To present Wrap each beignet in a few lettuce leaves, squeeze a little lime juice over, and eat in your fingers.

Smoked Trout Pâté

with Celery

Forget those heavy, dense pâtés crusted with butter and laden with fat: this one is as fresh and clean as a new spring day. Make it in minutes and serve in one big, or several little pots. Chill it well or even freeze it briefly before you set out.

Makes about 350g, Serves 8
Allow 45–50g per serving

To buy/find

250g boneless, skinless hot-smoked trout

1 teaspoon virgin olive oil

2 garlic cloves, chopped

1 tablespoon lemon juice

100g cream cheese or low fat soft cheese

1–2 teaspoons mild paprika

sea salt and freshly ground black pepper

2 tablespoons chopped fresh herbs e.g. dill, chives

2 celery hearts

To prepare/make Flake the trout into a food-processor or large mortar. Heat the olive oil in a frying pan and sauté the garlic briefly. Add the lemon juice. Spoon this in with the trout and process, or pound using a pestle. Add the soft cheese, paprika, seasonings and some of the herbs and process, in brief bursts, or pound briefly, to make a pink paste, with a slightly rough texture. Taste and adjust seasonings. Smooth into one large or several small, metal containers or china pots. Push a little fresh herb on top of each, and a little extra black pepper. Chill for 1 hour, or refrigerate for up to 4 days. Briefly freeze – say for 45 minutes – if the weather is hot and the journey long. Wash and shake dry the celery. Wrap it in wet kitchen paper or cloth and plastic. Chill it while the pâté chills. Take a knife for spreading.

To present Surround the trout pâté with some crisp, freshly cut lengths of celery.

29

Soups

Soups are suddenly having a renaissance and are, once again, funky and fun. 'Big bowl' cafés serving dumplings and noodles in hot broth, and juice bars which serve freshly squeezed, iced sweet or savoury juices (rather like iced soups – for example 'smoothies'), can be seen as part of the same story.

Hot soup is a salvation to anyone feeling cold, discouraged and in need of a boost. But ethnic, epicurean, chilled, sweet and even jellied soups exist as well: the scope is enormous and infinitely interesting. And soup is easily portable.

Gazpacho, Bouillabaisse, Congee, Caldo Verde, Consommé: such names summon up real magnificence. All of these are soups, all of them are famous. They sustain people the world over.

Be bold with whatever soup you serve. Soup should come very hot or icy cold. Few soups taste ideal when lukewarm, so do pack and organise accordingly. These days, with vacuum flasks, insulated containers and excellent cooking apparatus good for picnics, snack meals and barbecues, it's become easy to exploit their possibilities.

Apply the same creativity to the size of your soup servings: tiny cups, glasses or miniature china bowls can be perfect for certain soups. Others deserve to be presented in giant mugs, big earthy cups, generous bowls or heatproof tumblers.

The recipe ideas mentioned so far can be a basis for your own exploration. The favourite recipes found in this book include iced black bean soup with chipotle cream; carrot, orange and cardamom soup; borscht; green pea and prosciutto soup. You will also find miso soup containing *dashi* with noodles in the bento picnic box. These soups have flavour, colour, and in some cases, unusual textures. There is the fresh boost of chilli, herbs or spices or the sweet scent of prosciutto to add appeal. Although some of the soups are here served hot, you could equally well serve them cold.

Soups are very versatile, as long as you taste and season intelligently and garnish appropriately. But if you want them elegant or subtle, they can satisfy these requirements too. Of all the dishes in this book, these are some of the most easily made and enjoyed.

Enjoy soups on their own – as a feast in their own right, accompanied by some crusty bread and followed by fresh fruit – or as part of the menus suggested later.

Carrot, Orange & Cardamom Soup

An exotic, vivid, colourful and fragrant soup which can be made in a flash. Serve it hot or iced. The harissa, a red, spicy North African condiment, is delicious when home made (see page 69) and is also available from French and African stores, and good delis and supermarkets.

Makes 1.2 litres, Serves 4

To buy/find

500g large organic carrots

750ml chicken or vegetable stock, boiling

1/2 teaspoon sea salt flakes

1–2 teaspoons harissa (hot spicy) paste

20 green cardamom pods, crushed, plus 8 to garnish

2 oranges, scrubbed

1 small shallot, finely chopped

To prepare/cook Peel and thinly slice the carrots crosswise into a small saucepan. Add the hot stock, bring to boiling, and reduce to a lively simmer. Add the salt, harissa and black cardamom seeds removed from their green pods. Stir to mix. Now squeeze in the juice of the oranges. Use a grater or zester to remove 1/4–1/2 teaspoon of orange zest. Once the carrots are tender, 10–12 minutes, pour the pan contents plus the zest and shallot into a blender. Blend to a creamy soup. Heat to boiling, or chill thoroughly. Pour the soup into a vacuum flask and seal. Wrap up the extra cardamom pods and take along as well.

To present Use bowls, cups, *demitasse* cups or glasses for serving the soup. Savour the aroma, scattering on some extra cardamom seeds for pleasure just before drinking.

Green Pea & Prosciutto Soup

Real, fresh baby green peas in the pod are a brief luxury: they must be eaten within hours of picking. This recipe, using easily obtainable frozen petits pois, gives you the sweetness, colour, succulence and vitamins of fresh peas and it can be completed within 20 minutes. Serve it hot or cold, with some mellow cured Italian ham added at the end.

Makes 1.5 litres, Serves 8

To buy/find

25g butter, chopped

6 spring onions, green and white parts, sliced

50g new potatoes, scrubbed and sliced

750g pack frozen petits pois

500ml boiling water

250ml creamy milk

6 thin slices prosciutto di Parma (cured Italian ham)

salt and freshly ground white pepper

To prepare/cook Heat the butter in a saucepan and when sizzling add the spring onions and sliced potatoes. Fry for 1–2 minutes, stirring now and then. Add the peas and boiling water and bring the pan contents back to boiling. Cover the pan, reduce heat and cook for 8 minutes more. Add half the milk and half the pan contents to a blender. Blend until smooth. Pour out the blended soup. Now, to the blender, add the remaining milk, remaining pan contents and 2 of the ham slices, scissor-chopped. Blend again until smooth. Combine the two mixtures, stir, taste and season well. Reheat to boiling once again and pour into wide-mouthed vacuum flask and seal. Alternatively chill completely, then add several ice cubes and pour into the vacuum flask. Wrap the remaining prosciutto in waxed paper.

To present Pour out the soup, hot or cold, into big mugs, china cups or soup bowls. Pass soup spoons. Finger-shred the remaining prosciutto into each serving.

Iced Black Bean Soup

with Chipotle Cream

A Mexican-style soup and a beauty. If authentic dried black beans (not Chinese salted black beans) are hard to find, substitute several cans of good quality black beans instead: this saves hours.

Makes 1.5 litres, Serves 8

To buy/find

4 tablespoons corn oil

8 spring onions, chopped

4 garlic cloves, crushed

1 green jalapeño chilli, cored, deseeded, sliced

1 teaspoon ground cumin

2 teaspoons ground coriander

75g fresh coriander, chopped

2 tablespoons tomato purée

750g cooked or canned black beans *(frijoles negros)*

750ml boiling chicken stock

sea salt and freshly ground black pepper

To serve:

2 tablespoons chipotles *en escabèche*, or dried chipotles (smoked, dried jalapeños)

150ml thick cream

To prepare/cook Heat the oil, add the spring onions and sauté 2–3 minutes. Now add the garlic, green jalapeño, cumin, ground and fresh coriander, tomato purée and beans. Pour in the boiling stock. Bring the pan contents back to boiling. Simmer, uncovered, for 15 minutes or so. Blend the soup, in batches if necessary, until creamy. Return the soup to the pan. Stir, adjust seasonings and turn off the heat. Cool the soup over iced water. Chill in the refrigerator. Make the chipotle cream: if using chipotles *en escabèche*, simply chop or mash. If using dried chipotles, dry roast them briefly in a hot frying pan then soak briefly in hot water, simmer until soft, then chop or mash. Stir into the cream and pack separately. When the soup is cold, pour into one or two wide-mouthed vacuum flasks, adding 2 ice cubes to each.

To present Stir the chipotle cream into the soup at serving time.

Hot Borscht

with Rolls or Bagels

The best borscht I've tasted was in Moscow; the next best in the Marais, in Paris, but my own is opinionated and tasty. Raw beetroot works best: if unobtainable use cooked beets. Serve this soup with soured cream, crème fraîche or more abstemiously, with low-fat fromage frais. Rolls or bagels are a great accompaniment.

Makes 1.5 litres, Serves 8

To buy/find

1 tablespoon virgin olive oil

4 garlic cloves, chopped or crushed

1 red onion, sliced

1/8–1/4 fresh red chilli e.g. serrano, or habanero

1 carrot, thinly sliced

8g dried mushrooms e.g. ceps or morels, crumbled

600g fresh beetroot or cooked canned beets

1 litre boiling chicken stock

2–3 tablespoons red wine vinegar

salt and freshly ground black pepper

handful fresh coriander leaves, to garnish

To serve:

8 tablespoons soured cream, cream or low-fat fromage frais

8 crusty white rolls or bagels

To prepare/cook Combine the oil, garlic, onion, chilli, carrot and mushrooms in a saucepan. Cook, stirring, over high heat for 2 minutes. Peel, slice or cube the beetroot into the pan then add the boiling stock and most of the vinegar. Bring the pan contents back to boiling. Reduce heat, simmer for 15–20 minutes or until the beetroot is tender and flavours blended. Taste, add remaining vinegar if you like and add salt and pepper to balance. (If you prefer a smooth soup, blend the soup to a purée.) Pour the hot soup into a wide-mouthed vacuum flask. Seal tightly. Pack the herbs and cream or fromage frais separately in pots with secure lids. Pack cups, mugs or glasses or bowls.

To present Pour out portions of soup. Add a spoonful of cream, soured cream or fromage frais, and sprinkle with coriander leaves. Pass the rolls or bagels and enjoy.

Sandwiches & wraps

Food put between slices of bread, or rolled up inside salad leaves, flatbreads or rice-paper wraps can be really fun, truly portable, multicultural and completely delectable. It goes without saying that the ingredients must be at peak freshness: the fruits juicy, the salad leaves crisp, the seafood, charcuterie, meat or poultry perfect. Flavoured butters and spreads can add interest, good seasoning mixes or dressings give finesse.

Watercress Sandwiches *page 43*

Pa Am Tomaquet *page 46*

Lebanese Lamb Wraps *page 48*

A roll and some soup; bread and cheese; salad and some fresh fruit: these must be some of the best-known, and well-loved quick snacks, easily carried to another place. Food on the move: a sandwich could be said to be a perfect example of this. Yet, oddly, sandwiches are often consigned to the footnotes of cookery, not taken very seriously. This seems a pity: they are an eminently useful idea, and can be as exciting and varied as any main course dish.

There are hundreds of sandwich formats: from bruschetta to *bocadillos* – versions of which are included in this chapter. Sandwiches may be open or closed, small or large. They can be made using long French bread sticks or round crusty loaves, flat focaccia or ciabatta loaves, sourdough 'subs', wholegrain baps: the list is endless. They may be hearty or refined, spicy or mild.

Flat, layered sandwiches are not the only type: rolled-up sandwiches are a stylish alternative; a common sense solution to eating on the run, using fingers, not forks. Such roll-ups and wraps are found in the Middle East, in South East Asia and many other areas. The wrappers may be made of thin, flatbreads such as pitta; they may be made of flour tortillas. Sometimes the wraps are made of salad leaves for elegant, clean freshness. These may combine melon, peach or avocado with spicy or savoury foods: cured ham or hummus, for example, to create contrast and variety.

The best sandwiches are often created on site, using freshly bought bread, split open, and whatever local speciality – cheeses, pickles, pâtés, fish pastes, vegetable and spice spreads – is available and excellent. Some of these ideas are incorporated in Chapter 1.

Spreads matter, too, in sandwich making. Fresh butter, lovely olive oil, spreadable soft cheeses all work well. I have included several ideas for you to make your own flavoured butters.

If the chunkier breads are to be toasted or grilled, this must be done quickly: keeping the outside crisp, the inner crumb still soft. Drizzle on the best estate-bottled extra virgin olive oil.

Try to avoid using the kind of cottonwool breads which taste of nothing, or soften to a pulp. Choose crusty bread from your local bakery, or delicious ethnic breads. Next, have herbs and salads crisp, well-drained and cold; meats and seafood, egg products, cheeses and rice should be at the best, appropriate, safe temperature.

Depending upon the situation, packing, wrapping or organising 'make-on-the-spot' wraps and sandwiches need a little care and attention, so follow the lively suggestions here for good results.

Sandwiches are magnificent yet convenient portable feasts in miniature.

FLAVOURED BUTTERS

Throughout this book you'll find many flavoured butters – such the barbecue baste used with the prawns cooked for a beach barbecue. There is truffle butter (to go on hot noodles) and a butter 'mousse'. You will find chutney butter (with the ham and gherkin roll-ups) and ginger and citrus butter (part of crab and ginger sandwiches); these can be used in other dishes according to your own ideas.

Today, there is also a range of flavoured ready-made butters – such as garlic and herb butter – to use, and butters come in many varieties: salted, mildly salted, unsalted and lactic, such as some of the finest French types. There is organic butter and clarified butter, which cooks hot, clean and reduces splattering. Do not use substitutes apart from virgin olive oil.

Butter, used wisely, can boost the flavours and freshness of your meals. It means that your sandwiches are well stuck together: though spreadable when soft, butter keeps bread together firmly when sandwiches are wrapped, or in an insulated container.

Here is a list of ready-made items which, if beaten into a little softened butter, will be delicious additions to your portable feast:

Ligurian pesto, red pesto, tapénade, sun-dried tomato paste, garlic purée, lemongrass purée, ginger purée, anchovies (mashed to a paste), capers (chopped and mashed), grated *Parmigiano Reggiano* cheese, herbed Boursin cheese, grated Cheddar, Roquefort cheese, Gorgonzola cheese and Dolcelatte layered with basil, all easily mashed and included. Easiest of all: freshly crushed garlic and whatever herbs are tasty, available and in season. Even peanut butter, with a shake or two of chilli sauce and soy sauce, some softened butter and a few chopped spring onions or shreds of ginger can make plain flatbreads fascinating. Or add crumbled crisp bacon: peanut butter and bacon is, oddly enough, delicious.

Cheese, Ham & Salad-filled Mini Loaves

These are masterpieces of invention: fillings packed neatly into crusty rolls or tiny loaves with the top lids and crumb removed. The lid is then set back on top, sealing them for travelling. To eat they can be sliced into halves or quarters.

Serves 4

To buy/find

4 round or oval crusty rolls

6 tablespoons extra virgin olive oil

4 tablespoons fresh pesto (not pasteurised)

1 handful flatleaf parsley, chopped

8 slices prosciutto di Parma (cured Italian ham)

250g canned, roasted artichokes
or wild mushrooms in oil, drained

125g soft blue cheese, e.g. Gorgonzola, Roquefort,
Bleu d'Auvergne, Bleu de Bresse

16 dry-cured salted black olives, pitted,
or anchovy-stuffed green olives

To prepare/make Slice off and keep the lids of each roll. Set aside. Using a grapefruit knife, scoop out the crumbs, leaving an even, crusty wall or shell. Pile the crumbs into a food-processor along with half the olive oil, the pesto and parsley. Process in bursts, to get densely green fragrant crumbs. Use the remaining oil to brush inside each hollowed-out roll, including the interior of the lid. Spoon an eighth of the crumbs into each roll. Add a folded prosciutto slice. Add more crumbs and a quarter of the roasted artichokes or mushrooms and cheese. Push in the second prosciutto slice and 4 olives. Push the lid into place on top. Wrap tightly using waxed paper, plastic wrap or dampened cloth. Wedge them, upright, into a small box or basket.

To present Undo the wrappings. Let diners eat them whole, halved or quartered.

Note:

These little layered loaves are a version of the famous French recipe, pan bagnat, *usually made using a split, French stick, drizzled with olive oil and with similarly piquant filling, then squashed down hard (some experts suggest it should be sat upon) until flattened. These individual little loaves need no sitting on: in fact they're so durable that they should be able to withstand all sorts of rough treatment.*

Crusty Breads

with Spicy Peppers & *Jamon Serrano*

A 'bocadillo' is a sandwich – a well-loved snack found all over Spain. The tastes are delightful: the olive oil is invariably fruity and spicy and green; the cured meats superb and the pickles, preserves and beans wonderful. Make these sandwiches and dream of Seville or Bilbao. Drink a classy Rioja or Navarra wine to complete the image.

Serves 4

To buy/find

4 long bread rolls

5 tablespoons extra virgin olive oil

250g cooked white beans (canned,
or in jars from a good delicatessen)

4 garlic cloves, crushed

salt and freshly ground black pepper

8 thin slices *jamon serrano* (Spanish cured, mountain ham)

8–12 canned *piquillo* peppers (roasted, skinned,
spicy red peppers) or canned pimientos

To prepare/make Slice the rolls lengthwise almost in two but keep a hinge on each. Drizzle the interior crumb of each base with 2 teaspoons of the oil, almost 3 tablespoons in total. Mash 2 tablespoons of the remaining oil with the white beans, garlic, salt and pepper, to make a messy paste. A fork will do this perfectly well. Spoon a quarter of this bean paste along each roll. Fold in 2 slices of serrano ham to each. Pack 2 or 3 *piquillo* peppers on top. Now wrap each roll in a square of waxed paper or a colourful cloth. Pack into a basket, pannier or bag to transport.

To present Unwrap and eat.

Ham & Gherkin Roll-ups

Sweet, cooked ham, sharply piquant baby cocktail gherkins and chutney-flavoured butter, all rolled up inside soft white bread makes finger food for children (and the young in heart) which is easy and delicious. Find any excuse – these are enjoyable treats for any occasion: a picnic, tea party, trip to the grandparents, or to take in your back-pack when off on adventures to mountains and lakes. They are extremely convenient to pack.

Makes 16, Serves 4

To buy/find

8 thin slices very fresh white square 'tin' loaf

2 tablespoons salted butter, softened

1 tablespoon mango or other chutney, finely chopped

24 tiny cocktail cornichons (baby gherkins) or 1 large dill pickle, drained

8 slices cooked smoked ham

To prepare/make Pile the bread up high. Use a sharp, serrated knife to slice off and discard the crusts. Wrap the bread briefly in a dampened cloth, or spray with water. Meanwhile mix the soft butter with the chutney. Drain and dry the gherkins. If using a large dill pickle, slice lengthwise into 8 segments. Unwrap the bread. Line the slices up in a row. Using a spatula, rubber scraper or palette knife, coat the bread slices with the chutney-butter. Put each bread slice on a square of plastic wrap, and set a ham slice on each. Put 3 gherkins (end to end) or a dill pickle segment diagonally across each ham-covered bread slice. Now, starting at one corner, roll each slice up tightly. Place these, joins down, on the same dampened cloth, in two piles. Wrap up neatly. Pack inside a plastic box or bag. Take a sharp, preferably folding, knife.

To present Cut across, at an angle, giving 16 roll-ups, and remove plastic wrap. Perfect to eat in your fingers!

Watercress Sandwiches

Somehow this brings to mind childhood simplicity. Ensure that the cress is very clean, the butter at a spreading temperature and the bread soft.

Makes 24 small sandwiches, Serves 4

To buy/find

12 slices thin white square 'tin' loaf

75g salted butter, softened

2 tablespoons thick mayonnaise

2 teaspoons boiling water

1 bunch or 2 x 85g packs watercress or cress, washed

freshly ground black pepper

salad leaves, e.g. Webb's Wonder, to garnish

To prepare/make Spread out the bread into two lines, edges touching, so that it makes one rectangle. Whisk the butter with the mayonnaise, and the boiling water: you should obtain a mousse-like cream. Use a wide-bladed spatula or rubber scraper to smooth the butter-mousse across all the bread slices, right to the edges. Shake the cress dry. Pull or snip off the cress sprigs and press them on the buttered surfaces of half the slices so they are well covered. Sprinkle with black pepper to taste. Lay a buttered slice face down on a cress-covered slice; pile up the sandwiches into a tower. Pressing down evenly, use a sharp, serrated knife to slice off and discard the crusts. Leave the sandwiches whole. Use waxed paper, plastic wrap or a wet cotton table napkin to wrap the sandwiches tightly in a neat block. Take the same sharp, serrated knife to the picnic site along with a lettuce, washed and wrapped in dampened cloth or plastic.

To present Unwrap the sandwiches. Slice into four triangles, squares or fingers. Arrange as liked on a plate, basket or tray on a bed of salad leaves.

Crab & Ginger Sandwiches

I first tasted these, or something similar, at a party. We sipped wine and a waiter carried around a handsome sourdough loaf inside which, like treasures, we found fine, tiny little sandwiches. You can vary the filling (e.g. smoked salmon could be an alternative) but keep the concept similar: it's impressive, portable and certainly a stylish feast.

Serves 8 or more

To buy/find

1 large 'boule' (round shaped) sourdough or whole wheat loaf (about 850g)

1 lemon or lime

75g salted butter, softened

2.5cm piece fresh root ginger, scrubbed

400g prepared, cooked crabmeat, lobster or smoked salmon

3 tablespoons thick mayonnaise or hollandaise sauce

1/8 teaspoon cayenne pepper

sea salt and freshly ground black pepper

To prepare/make Slice off a top 'lid' from the loaf; set it aside. Using a short, sharp, serrated knife, make a vertical cut, about 1cm in from the crust, all the way round and nearly to the base. Cut a line across the centre of the crumb to make two semi-circles. Using your fingers, carefully lift out a semi-circular 'plug' of bread. Repeat on the other side. Trim the bases of these bread chunks to make them smooth. Turn the pieces of crumb flat side down, and, using an electric carving knife or long sharp, serrated knife, slice each thinly into 6 or 8 thin layers. Stack in 2 piles, in the shape of the original chunks, and cover with a dampened cloth. Squeeze a little lemon or lime and grate a little zest, finely, into the butter. Using a ginger grater or fine metal grater, grate the ginger, skin and all. Scrape the pulp into the butter. In a bowl, break up the crabmeat with a fork, add the mayonnaise and seasonings. Beat well until smooth. Unwrap the bread. Butter 2 bread slices and spread on a share of crab filling. Press the sandwich closed. Repeat until all the bread, butter and filling are used up, and wrap once again in the damp cloth for 10–30 minutes. Unwrap. Stack the finished sandwiches in the same chunks again, and insert each carefully in the hollow loaf. Slice the sandwiches across, inside the hollowed-out loaf crust, to make quarters, and again to make triangles. Set the lid on top of the loaf at an angle or else on top, as normal. Wrap the entire loaf in plastic wrap or foil.

To present On site, unwrap the loaf and place on a cloth-covered tray. Allow friends to push or lift the lid and help themselves.

Pa Am Tomaquet

In Catalonia, northern Spain, this famous and delicious snack seems as usual as pizza does in Naples. It consists of local produce: chunky bread, grilled or griddled, rubbed with a smashed garlic clove then with a crushed ripe tomato. Salt is usually added, but the final flourish is a generous libation of good, fresh local extra virgin olive oil: a tomato sandwich which is a triumph of simplicity, ease and freshness. This can be created on site, as long as there is a portable barbecue, or, more romantically, a little wood fire – even a tiny portable camping gas element can make toast, with a rack to set on top.

Serves 4

To buy/find

4 chunks bread from a crusty country loaf

4 garlic cloves, skin on

4 large ripe, juicy tomatoes

sea salt

estate-bottled, extra virgin olive oil, for drizzling

To prepare/cook Take the gear needed for a fire on the spot: portable barbecue, gas-fired element or aromatic wood. Get the relevant equipment to the heated temperature or build the fire to hot and crackling. Toast the bread, both sides, over the heat. Crush each garlic clove and use it to rub garlic all over one side of the toast. Now rub squashy tomato flesh over too; if it looks pink and messy: par for the course. Add salt to taste and a generous trickle of oil.

To present Eat each sandwich while warm, aromatic and crusty. You may add more salt and oil to the tomato debris and eat that too.

Ewe's Milk Cheese on Bruschetta

Long before bruschetta became fashionable everywhere it was a peasant dish from the Abruzzi, in Italy, designed to maximise the pleasure of tasting the new season's olive oil. *Fettunta* is the Tuscan version. Chunks of homely bread are toasted or chargrilled briefly then rubbed with garlic and sprinkled lavishly with the best olive oil available. In this version, pecorino is added. Some wild greens – dandelion, radish, cress, rocket or wild garlic leaves, if available – can also be added. A portable mini-feast, all of its own.

Serves 4

To buy/find

4 thick slices Italian-style bread e.g. *pane integrale*

4 garlic cloves, squashed

cold, first-pressed extra virgin olive oil, to taste

250g pecorino cheese or other ewe's milk cheese

wild, fresh herbs such as dandelion, radish, cress, rocket or wild garlic (optional)

sea salt

To prepare/cook On site, fire up a portable barbecue, make a small wood fire (if it is safe) or heat a gas-fired element. Barbecue, toast or grill the bread on a rack over the heat. Use the garlic to rub all over one side of the crusty bread, then drizzle on oil directly from the bottle, flask or can. Add some slices of cheese and some wild herbs. (Note: Do rinse them thoroughly under some bottled spring water to clean them well.) Sprinkle with salt to taste.

To present Hand around the ready-made open sandwiches.

Lebanese Lamb Wraps

In the Middle East lamb *kibbeh* may be presented either raw or cooked. In this version it is cooked and, instead of cracked wheat, I use couscous which adds an interesting texture. Make the *kibbeh* just before you want to eat and serve them fresh and hot, or alternatively make them ahead and chill or even freeze them. They still taste excellent defrosted and heated well using a steamer, microwave or moderate oven. Alternatively serve them cold. Lavash is a flat bread, easy to roll up. Find it in Iranian and Lebanese grocers; but rotis, pitta breads or even flour tortillas could be substituted; not authentic but never mind – neither is the couscous!

Serves 4

To buy/find

500g twice-minced good quality lean lamb

2 tablespoons spice mix such as Chermoula, 'Ali Berberé' (see page 68)

1 teaspoon celery salt

1 handful parsley, chopped

100g 'instant' couscous

100ml boiling stock or water

2 garlic cloves, chopped

2 tablespoons freshly squeezed lemon juice

1 handful fresh mint, chopped

To serve:

4 thin lavash flat breads (or roti, pitta or tortillas)

100g pre-soaked, pitted dried apricots

extra flatleaf parsley sprigs

8–12 Cos lettuce leaves (outer ones)

100g *hummus bi tahini* (chickpea and tahini paste) (see page 22) (optional)

To prepare/cook Mix the lamb, spice mix, celery salt and parsley together. Leave to stand, covered, in a cool place. Mix the couscous with the boiling stock, garlic, lemon juice and, once it has cooled, the mint. Leave until cold. Drain off any excess liquid. Then add the lamb, using clean hands, and knead it all well together. Divide into 12. Shape each into a torpedo-shaped *kibbeh*, smoothing off the ends. Cook these by baking in an oven preheated to 180°C for 20–25 minutes or microwave them, six at a time, on High (750 watts) for 3 minutes, turning them over after 2 minutes. If you prefer, grill (8–10 minutes, turning) or barbecue (about 10 minutes).

To present Wrap each *kibbeh* in a wrap of flat bread, adding some apricot halves, parsley, Cos leaves and a blob, if you like, of ready-made *hummus bi tahini*. Eat in the fingers.

Prosciutto & Treviso Wraps

These are a miracle of ease and style. Select crisp, pretty Italian salad leaves. Keep them intact and, on site, roll them up around a twist of fine fragrant prosciutto di Parma, one of the world's most delicious of foods, and some freshly sliced melon (ogen, galia and cantaloupe are excellent).

Serves 4–6

To buy/find

4 heads *radicchio de trevise* or *ceriolo verde* radicchio (red chicory), or 2 of each

12 slices prosciutto di Parma (cured Italian ham)

1 ripe, scented whole rock or musk melon

fresh peppercorns, in a pepper grinder

To prepare/make Wash the salad head but leave it intact. Leave the prosciutto on its waxed paper, rolled up loosely. Take the whole, washed melon.

To present On site, set out all the components in a cloth-lined hamper or basket and add a pile of plates. Cut up the melon, removing skin and seeds. Participants pull off one or two leaves of radicchio, add a slice of ham, a sliver of melon and a few grinds of pepper. It is then rolled up and eaten.

Vietnamese Rice-paper Wraps

These delicacies are best assembled on the spot by each participant. Take along the packet of rice-paper sheets, a flask of warm water to soften them, the fillings and the dips. Duck breast scented with 5-spice powder, crisp raw vegetables and fresh mint go inside. Salted peanut garnish and one or two dips complete the presentation. The process of making these snacks, which taste fresh and crisp and pungent, is fun and democratic – make them as thin or as well-filled as you like.

Serves 6

To buy/find

2 *magrets de canard* (Barbary duck breasts), smoked

1 teaspoon 5-spice powder

1 teaspoon dark soy sauce

1 x 350g pack triangular or round Vietnamese rice wrappers (*Bahn Trang*)

Fillings and serving stuffs:

1 carrot, in long shreds

4 spring onions, in long shreds

250g daikon or mooli radish, peeled, in long strips

100g bean sprouts

2 red peppers, deseeded, in long strips

50g fresh mint or Vietnamese mint sprigs

1 Cos lettuce, washed but whole

125ml hoisin sauce, yellow bean sauce or plum sauce

75g roasted, salted peanuts, chopped

125ml sweet chilli sauce (Chinese type)

125ml *nuoc cham* sauce (see page 99)

To prepare/cook Rub the smoked duck breasts all over with the spice and the soy. Bake in an oven preheated to 200°C for 30–40 minutes or until brown, juicy and aromatic. Pack the prepared salad fillings and the whole lettuce into one large plastic snap-top container or zip-top bags or clip-top bowls, checking they are wetted well first to retain crispness. Pack the hoisin sauce, peanuts, chilli sauce and *nuoc cham* into small, separate snap-top tubs or clip-top bowls. Keep the rice wrappers dry and separated. Slice or shred the cooked, smoked duck into yet another sealed container, or foil. Take a vacuum flask of warm water for softening the rice wrappers, also an unbreakable flat dish, bowl or tray for this process, and a basting brush.

To present Unwrap and display all the various components. Pour out the warm water into the bowl for the diners to dip, rest and soften each rice wrap. The alternative is to paint one side with water, using a basting brush, until it softens. Shake each one free from drips. Take a lettuce leaf as a plate and place a wrapper on it. Spread the wrap with some hoisin, yellow bean sauce or plum sauce. Add some duck then some salad stuffs. Roll up the wrap, tucking in the ends if you feel the need. Now dip each wrap first into a dipping sauce, then into some peanuts. Eat it: leaf 'plate', wrap and all. Continue until all ingredients have been used up.

Barbecue

"Let's have a barbecue": this always seems a welcome invitation. Images of relaxed, animated conversation, warm midday sun or the gentle fading light of dusk, with a tall, icy refreshing drink in your hand and the enticing smell of smoke, the sizzle and hiss as food cooks, all seem utterly appealing. Barbecues arouse appetites in an uniquely enjoyable way.

Mexican barbecue *page 56*

Clambake *page 60*

Country barbecue *page 64*

Outdoor cooking over a wood or charcoal fire is about the most ancient of cooking methods. It lends to the cooked food a uniquely appetite-arousing, smoky savour. It also arouses a sense of adventure.

Barbecues, a passion in recent years, are an easy way to entertain a number of people in a relaxed and informal way. Fun is assured, whatever the weather.

Cooking over fire can now apply to wheeled chrome and steel barbecue trolleys with gas bottles set beneath, or a barbecue fashioned at home from a metal box, some bricks and some chicken-wire. A wood fire on the beach, with a grid arranged on some stones, can also cook food over the embers.

Today humble disposable barbecues are common in petrol-station forecourts and from home-improvement stores. Some simple but enduring designs, such as the Japanese barbecues with levers to suspend the barbecue rack at different heights, continue to be used and loved. Recently, domed outdoor ovens have become available which can roast or barbecue.

Barbecue disasters mainly stem from the lack of understanding that the best cooking is done once the flames have died down and the embers are at a steady, gentle, ashy glow. This is the ideal. Cooking is not immediate: so allow for this and have interesting easy snacks to enjoy and drinks to sip while the foods are cooking in their own time. Anticipation sharpens the appetite!

Setting the food an appropriate distance from the heat – so that the inside cooks in the time it takes to sizzle, but not char the exterior – is the other important consideration. With a little experience it is easy to learn these things.

Another concern is that too-sugary coatings, though often tasty, can cook too quickly and become too dark. Use these recipes as a basic guide and do not overdo things. Evenly sized food can also help to make the cooking process error free. Flattening some foods may help; sometimes threading foods on to skewers is the best solution to ensure even cooking.

Charred food is inedible (potentially carcinogenic, too) but grossly under-cooking meat, poultry or fish can not only be unappetising but a real health risk: proper cooking will inactivate micro-organisms that could cause illness. Another safety issue; many enthusiasts will take a fire blanket to the scene and keep it nearby; others swear by a small portable fire extinguisher – either is a practical choice.

Some experts insist that if you cook over an open wood fire, you should dig a little trench all around the area of your fire to ensure that any plant roots cannot smoulder and later burn: at any rate, pouring cold water over the fire before you leave is a responsible move. Digging a pit about 15cm deep or removing sand or stones to this depth then building your fire inside this pit is another sensible idea.

Check that the metal parts of any barbecue are of chrome-plated steel and rust resistant. Have a bucket of cold water near at hand to put out any unwanted fires. Pack suitable foods, prepared and raw, lots of hot and cold drinks, packs of ice in insulated containers, kitchen paper, napkins, charcoal, your portable barbecue (or the makings for your wood fire), tools, and then be off. Cushions, umbrellas and some sunscreen are important too. Once the meal is under way, enthusiasm and enjoyment will be guaranteed!

Mexican barbecue

Mexico has a vivid appeal. Revel in some of its spicy, herbal chilli-enhanced flavours, its earthy, colourful dishes, and its easy conviviality by creating this barbecue or *parilla* menu. Add some margaritas, open some beers, hang up paper lanterns and light candles: it's fiesta time.

Chicken Fajitas

with Salad

Fajitas – traditionally made with strips of beef in a marinade – are made with wheat, not maize tortillas and are a favourite at any gathering. This cross-cultural version uses chicken. For a beach *parilla* (barbecue) for a crowd make it simple. These fajitas are do-it-yourself: this makes it fun for all and not merely hard work for the cooks. The four-skewer system for holding the quickly-cooked chicken is foolproof: try it. There is no waiting as all the chicken is ready at the same time.

Serves 8

To buy/find

450g can red beans, mashed

250ml barbecue-tomato sauce

500g guacamole (see page 22) or bought guacamole

450ml soured cream

450g low-fat soft cheese, crumbled or sliced

16 wheat flour tortillas

2 teaspoons fresh red chilli, sliced

6 tablespoons sun-dried tomato paste or tomatillo purée

4 tablespoons corn oil

8 boneless chicken breasts, sliced lengthwise into 6

1 large handful fresh coriander leaves

4 fresh limes, in chunky pieces

To prepare/cook Mash the drained red beans, either before you set out or on site, in their can using a fork, and adding the barbecue-tomato sauce to make a thick bean purée. Put the mashed beans, guacamole, soured cream and the cheese in separate bowls or containers which can be passed around. Have the tortillas covered, maybe in baskets or between cloths, near to the barbecue ready for being warmed and filled.

To make the coating for the chicken: mix the chopped fresh red chilli together with the tomato paste or tomatillo purée, mixing in the corn oil. Toss the chicken strips in the chilli mixture until coated. Line up 24 chicken strips in a parallel row. Using 2 long skewers, thread the strips on to the skewers like the rungs of a ladder: they can now be lifted as one unit. Repeat with the remaining chicken strips and 2 more skewers. Set these 'chicken ladders' over the *parilla* (barbecue) and cook for 3–4 minutes on each side, until the chicken is firm and white inside.

To present Pull out the skewers and let guests fill their tortillas with chicken, coriander and the accompaniments of their choice. Squeeze a little lime juice over.

Roasted Sweetcorn

and Spiced Butter

Mexico taught me to appreciate sweetcorn and its potential. Roasting or barbecuing it directly over the heat, still in its wetted husks, then sizzling it with spices makes this homely vegetable seem delectable, new and exciting.

Serves 8

To buy/find

3–4 garlic cloves, crushed

50g salted butter, softened

2 teaspoons smoky paprika, Spanish-style

8 whole sweetcorn cobs, husks and silks still intact

To prepare/cook Mix together the garlic, butter and paprika and set aside. Gently pull open the green husks and silks a little and drip some cold water inside each cob – about 1 tablespoon will be enough for each. Set them over a prepared barbecue, 5–7.5cm from the embers or closer. Cook them over the heat, turning them with tongs or fingers from time to time, for 10–20 minutes or until steamy and semi-tender. Now pull the dampened husks and silks back completely to reveal the kernels. Replace the corn cobs on the barbecue. As the kernels char and darken, add about a teaspoon of the spiced butter in little dots along the length of each cob. Let it melt and drip. Once the corn cobs look frizzled and charred dark in patches, remove them and add a share of the remaining spiced butter.

To present Eat, in the fingers, while still hot, leaving on the husks for holding.

To eat
Iced black bean soup with chipotle cream *page 34*
Roasted sweetcorn and spiced butter
Chicken fajitas with salad
Watermelon and fresh lime
To drink
Margaritas *page 125* and/or iced beer
Vanilla coffee *page 120*

57

Beach barbecue

Imagine a fire and the sound of waves. Now add lemons, prawns, spicy harissa paste, goat's cheese sizzling over potatoes; a green salad; all followed by ripe peaches flamboyantly cooked in cognac and Cointreau. These are grand and epicurean flavours but the setting can be wonderfully relaxed. Much of this food is cooked on site, with a few additions from your storecupboard. This superb menu celebrates summer at the beach.

> **To eat**
> Skewered prawns with harissa
> Potato and cheese salad *page 97*
> Green salad *page 94*
> Flambéed peaches
> **To drink**
> Chilled Chardonnay

Skewered Prawns

with Harissa

Harissa and herb butter make these king prawns or big shrimp on sticks very succulent and somewhat hot and spicy. If you cannot find raw prawns use ready-cooked ones instead: reheat rather than cook, using the same spicy butter, but for a shorter time.

Serves 8

To buy/find

1–2kg (16) large prawns in the shell (about 18cm long)

50g harissa spice paste (see page 69)

100g garlic butter or parsley butter, softened (bought or made)

4 lemons, cut in half, to serve

To prepare/cook Holding each prawn down flat on a cutting surface, use a sharp, serrated blade knife to cut the tail sections part-way through while leaving the head sections whole. The tail will divide into two, butterflying it. Discard the dark vein if you find it. Mash the harissa with the flavoured butter. Use 1–2 teaspoons per prawn and coat the exposed tail surfaces of each. Thread the prawns in twos or fours on to long metal skewers, looping them round to fit as necessary. Place the completed skewers over the glowing embers of the open fire, towards the cooler edge, or else rest them on a metal rack over the flames themselves. Once the shells turn rosy, brittle and aromatic and the flesh white and firm, they are cooked.

To present Present the skewers with the remaining harissa butter in small pots, for individual use, and pass each diner a lemon half. Have lots of paper or cloth napkins for messy, spicy fingers. Toss the shells on to the fire with the lemon skins to burn to cinders. They continue to smell delicious and it also avoids messy clearing up at the end.

Flambéed Peaches

with cognac and Cointreau

The colour of this deliciously scented dish complements the other elements of this bonfire banquet perfectly. Try to buy peaches that are fully ripe or buy them in advance and ripen them in a warm place. This is a bold but messy dish and utterly appealing.

Serves 8

To buy/find

16 small or 8 large ripe, scented peaches (2–3kg)

2 oranges

4–8 tablespoons clear honey

250ml cognac, or more to taste

250ml Cointreau (triple sec), or more to taste

To prepare/cook Halve the peaches by scoring around the circumference, twisting them and removing the pits. Heat the peach halves in 2 large frying pans over a corner of the fire (you may want to use old frying pans for this as the flames may discolour them slightly). Tear or cut the oranges in half and squeeze the juice over the peaches; trickle the honey over. Add the orange halves to the pan, if you like, for extra flavour. When the peaches are warmed through and juicy, warm a large metal ladle and half fill with cognac, then top up with Cointreau. Stir to mix. Hold the ladle near the heat and carefully ignite the contents with a long match or taper. Pour it, still flaming, over the peaches.

To present Spoon the peaches and their liquid into pretty dishes and eat immediately.

Clambake

This clambake menu is celebratory: lobsters, shellfish and succulent steamed vegetables all cooked in an 'earth oven' created by digging a pit in the sand, fire-heating stones, then closing the top. Trapped steam, inside, cooks the food. It is awe-inspiring.

Pit-cooked Lobsters, Prawns & Clams

(Clambake)

East Coast American summer clambakes are an old idea. They can be done in a number of ways. In Cape Cod people even have ingenious ways to recreate them in the kitchen in the dead of winter. But the classic system, when at the beach, is to dig a pit in the sand, line it with stones, and build an efficient fire in the pit. The food to be cooked is placed on a number of fine chicken-wire 'trays' which are then lowered on to the hot stones, often between layers of wetted seaweed, wetted leaves or samphire. The biggest foods go in first. As the steam works its way up it cooks the food to perfection. Don't expect it be done in minutes: it takes some hours. This is all part of the fun. Have palmiers to nibble, sun tea or soft drinks, beer, spritzers or white wine to drink until the main course is revealed.

Serves 8

To buy/find

8 x 500g live lobsters

wetted samphire or seaweed, to cook

4 sweet potatoes, unpeeled

4 onions, unpeeled (optional)

2 x 500g butternut squash, cut across into 5cm slices

2 quarts clams, scrubbed

2 quarts fresh, live mussels, scrubbed

8 jumbo prawns

salt and freshly ground black pepper

500g salted butter, melted or 500ml extra virgin olive oil, to serve

lemons (optional)

To prepare/cook First, get permission to build a fire if necessary. If possible, take a table to the site. Now dig a pit 1 metre by 75cm in area, and about 15–20cm deep, in the sand. Line the base and sides of the pit with non-fracturing large stones. Make a fire with wooden kindling and charcoal in the pit and let it burn for 1–2 hours to heat the stones thoroughly. Have at least 2 pieces of fine chicken-wire cut slightly longer than the size of the pit, with the ends rolled to make 'handles' for lifting. If you prefer, kill each live lobster humanely: hold it down carefully, and pierce through the head with a sharp, heavy knife. Scrub the lobsters briefly in a bucket of sea or spring water. When the stones are well heated and the fire has burned down, push the embers to one side. Place one chicken-wire 'tray' on the stones and cover with half the wetted samphire or seaweed. Place the lobsters on top with the sweet potatoes, onions (if used) and squash. Add the second layer of chicken-wire then the clams, mussels and prawns. Cover with the remaining wetted samphire or seaweed and a double layer of foil to act as a lid. Put large clean stones on top to keep the heat in. Leave the clambake to cook for 2–3 hours or even longer. Uncover one side a little and test the food: it should be hot and cooked through.

To present Arrange the cooked food on several large platters, including the samphire which is edible, and let the diners help themselves. Eat. Enjoy the foods dipped into the seasonings and then bowls of melted butter or olive oil. Lemons are an option.

City barbecue

All over the world people have devised portable, earthenware barbecue systems. In Tunisia and Greece, the ceramic barbecues are knee-high with a perforated grid inside for charcoal and an opening where ashes are removed. Indian tandoor-type ovens on metal stands are widely available these days: they make this sort of cooking easy and fun.

Flower Pot Chicken

A friend, whose inner city garden has no space for a formal barbecue, intrigued me by barbecuing on his front steps: cooking food on a metal grill set over glowing charcoal, arranged on broken bricks inside a large earthenware flower pot, about 45cm across. Ingenious – however, any barbecue will do.

Serves 8

To buy/find

8 small boneless chicken breasts

1 tablespoon sweet chilli sauce (Chinese type)

2 tablespoons virgin olive oil

2 teaspoons finely shredded lemon zest

1 tablespoon freshly squeezed lemon juice

8 juniper berries, well crushed or chopped

To prepare/cook Pat the chicken dry. Make 2 shallow long cuts in the thickest parts of the chicken so it will cook evenly. Mix together the sauce, olive oil, lemon zest, lemon juice and juniper berries. Rub this over the chicken in a shallow, non-reactive dish, turning the pieces in it to coat them. Get the flower-pot barbecue to the right heat. Set the chicken, skin-side down, and cook over a moderate heat for 6–8 minutes each side or until the chicken is firm, white and the juices run clear and golden, not pink.

To present Serve hot. Eat in the fingers or using a knife and fork.

Chargrilled Vegetables, Halloumi & Garlicky Toasts

In this recipe, the barbecued bread has a Mediterranean feel. Halloumi is a dense, mild Cypriot cheese often available from Greek or Cypriot delis. Raw it is innocuous, even dull, but grilled it has considerable charm. Cook over a second barbecue to accompany the chicken or cook them once the chicken is done, since lukewarm chicken tastes sticky and appealing. Griddled breads, cheese and vegetables taste better hot.

Serves 8

To buy/find

8 garlic cloves, unpeeled and crushed

6 tablespoons extra virgin olive oil

8 large flat field or portobello-type mushrooms

4 courgettes, halved lengthwise

1 aubergine, sliced crosswise into 1cm rounds

2 small bunches cherry tomatoes on the vine

375g halloumi cheese, cut into 8 slices

1 ciabatta, split lengthwise and cut crosswise into 8, or 1 focaccia, cut into 8 wedges

sea salt flakes and freshly ground black pepper

1 small handful fresh flatleaf parsley, to serve

To prepare/cook Peel 2 of the garlic cloves and mash up in the olive oil. Drizzle, paint or rub some of this garlicky olive oil over both sides of the mushrooms, courgettes, aubergine and over the tomatoes and halloumi. Have the fire at a good even temperature but not too fierce. Chargrill or barbecue the vegetables and halloumi for 3–5 minutes each side until tender and aromatic, even if they look somewhat collapsed. Push them to one side of the barbecue. Cook the bread slices until hot and smoky and lightly toasted. Rub and mash the 4 remaining crushed garlic cloves all over the bread to give it extra pungency. Drizzle the remaining garlicky olive oil over the toasted bread, sprinkle some of the parsley over.

To present Serve each piece of garlicky bread with a slice of grilled halloumi on top and some of the vegetables; season with salt and pepper. Serve with the Flower Pot Chicken (see left) and the remaining parsley.

To eat

Green pea and prosciutto soup
page 32

Flower pot chicken

Chargrilled vegetables,
halloumi and garlicky toasts

Greengages

To drink

Chilled Riesling

Elderflower tea *page 118*

Country barbecue

Baked Salmon & *Wasabi*

Effortless, easy salmon with no bones, skin or debris, seasoned with *wasabi* and chilli oil: faint Far Eastern touches which suit this occasion well since crab and ginger sandwiches also feature on this menu. If you prefer Japanese seaweed to baby spinach, *hijiki* is an alternative: buy it dry from wholefood or Japanese grocers. It plumps up when simmered in boiling water for 5–10 minutes.

Serves 8

To buy/find

2kg tail portion salmon, skinned and boned, prepared weight about 1.4kg

3 tablespoons chilli oil

2 tablespoons ready mixed *wasabi* (green horseradish) paste

2 teaspoons light soy sauce or fish sauce

100g baby spinach or 50g dried *hijiki* seaweed

To prepare/cook Pat the salmon dry on kitchen paper. Tear off a sheet of heavy duty foil; it should be more than twice the size of a salmon portion. Make a fold across halfway, so a salmon portion would sit comfortably in one half with a space all round. Paint or rub a tablespoon of the chilli oil over the upper side of the foil. Set one fillet, boned side up, on one half of the oiled foil. Rub on half the *wasabi*, half the soy. Cover with the baby spinach. If using *hijiki* seaweed, simmer it in about 250ml of boiling water until it plumps up and softens. Drain. Spread this over the fillet. Paint or rub the remaining *wasabi* and fish soy over the boned surface of the second salmon fillet. Set this, coated side down, on top of the first fillet, to recreate the salmon's natural shape. Trickle the remaining chilli oil all over the top. Fold the foil over to enclose the salmon and roll and crimp all the open edges to make a neat rectangular package. Set this package on some cloths so it does not get punctured, and take it to the site. Once the barbecue is at the correct heat, not too fierce, set the parcel above it and leave to cook for 12–20 minutes on each side, turning it over by the edges. Uncover carefully and check doneness; serve slightly underdone or according to taste.

To present Leave the salmon in its wraps: simply roll the foil back to reveal the fish. Let diners help themselves.

Why not prepare some stylish sandwiches, packed snug in their own sourdough loaf container; some rice salad; take some filletted salmon, asparagus, tomatoes and two portable barbecues and head off for the country? On site willing helpers can cook the fish and the vegetables; others assemble the dessert. This is a wonderful menu for any occasion.

Chargrilled Asparagus with Fontina & Garlicky Tomatoes

Ready-seasoned baby tomatoes and asparagus with melted cheese, hot from the barbecue, make a delicious accompaniment to open-air feasts.

Serves 8

To buy/find

1kg (2 generous bunches) plump green asparagus

2 small bunches of cherry or mini plum-type tomatoes, on the vine

4 garlic cloves, cut into long slivers

extra virgin olive oil (infused with basil if you like)

sea salt flakes and freshly ground black pepper

250g fontina, Gruyère or Emmenthal cheese, in 1cm cubes

To prepare/cook Snap off any tough stems from the asparagus. Blanch it briefly in a large frying pan of boiling water; drain and plunge into a bowl of iced water. Drain. Make a small hole near the top stem area of each tomato and push a sliver of garlic into each. Drizzle some olive oil over the asparagus and tomatoes to coat, and sprinkling with salt and pepper. Arrange the tomatoes and asparagus on a fine metal rack and barbecue until the tomatoes are wrinkled, hissing and sizzling: 3–4 minutes, turning the asparagus spears with tongs. Remove the tomatoes by the stems and snip each bunch into four. Roll the asparagus spears close together and sprinkle the cubed cheese on top. Part cover the asparagus with some foil or a pan lid until the cheese has melted.

To present Add another trickle of olive oil and salt and pepper to the tomatoes, and serve the asparagus, with its runny cheese, straight from the barbecue. Eat both in your fingers, taking care not to burn your mouth.

To eat

Crab and ginger sandwiches *page 44*

Baked salmon and *wasabi*

Chargrilled asparagus with fontina and garlicky tomatoes

Wild rice salad *page 100*

Raspberry fool with meringues *page 113*

To drink

Chilled Sancerre

Armagnac and coffee

Backyard barbecue

Hot Beef Satays

with Herbs

These quick beef satays have a subtly sweet Asian savour. They take moments to prepare – a brief time to cook. Garnish them with fresh herbs at serving time, such as Thai basil or European basil.

Serves 8

To buy/find

4 tablespoons canned coconut milk

2 tablespoons dark soy sauce

1 tablespoon dark soft brown sugar

10cm fresh lemongrass, thinly sliced crosswise

4 red or green bird's eye chillies, sliced

2 teaspoons freshly puréed garlic

2 teaspoons grated fresh root ginger

675g rump, sirloin or blade steak, in 1cm cubes

1 handful Thai basil or European basil, torn

To prepare/cook Soak 16 short satay sticks or bamboo or wood skewers in water while the satay ingredients are prepared. Mix together the first 7 ingredients to make the marinade. Thread equal amounts of beef cubes on the skewers. Set these on a shallow, non-reactive plate. Pour the marinade over. Turn the satays once and leave for at least 5 minutes. Barbecue over glowing embers or chargrill for about 2 minutes each side, basting with the marinade, until golden outside but still slightly rosy inside.

To present Eat hot or cool, scattered with basil.

Variation

Substitute chicken breast for the steak, if you like; add 1/2 teaspoon turmeric (optional) and use light soy sauce instead of dark.

Easy, backyard barbecues, in summer or autumn, including one or two simple, gourmet additions needing no cooking whatsoever, can create a relaxed ambiance. It helps if you can buy the oysters ready-opened, that your cheesemonger has ripe, trickling cheese on hand, and that juicy, fragrant, sweet pears are in season. The beef satays and skewered potatoes are up to you. Enjoy!

Skewered Potatoes

An easy, tasty idea made simpler by having the baby new potatoes part-cooked before they are barbecued. The crusty, crunchy outsides are really tempting. If you can, cook the new season potatoes for this dish the day before the barbecue and refrigerate them.

Serves 8

To buy/find

2kg new season baby potatoes, scrubbed

75g salted butter, softened

2 tablespoons extra virgin olive oil

2 tablespoons clear honey

4 spring onions, finely chopped

sea salt flakes and roughly crushed black pepper

To prepare/cook Boil or steam the baby potatoes until barely cooked and still firm. Drain. Have at least 8 flat metal skewers ready. Push an equal number of potatoes on to each skewer. Mix together the butter, oil, honey and half the spring onions. Dab or brush this all over the skewered potatoes. Cook them, at a reasonable distance from the heat source, for 3–5 minutes each side or until golden and crusty. It may take a little longer.

To present Sprinkle the remaining spring onions, the sea salt and pepper on top, and serve.

To eat
Smoked trout pâté with celery *page 29*
Hot beef satays with herbs
Skewered potatoes
Munster with pears *page 109*
To drink
Cabernet-Merlot
Armagnac and coffee

Barbecue marinades

These spicy, aromatic mixtures, both dry and wet, can be used to give a lively, ethnic-style flavour boost to many basic barbecue recipes. Rub them in, sprinkle them over, use them as coatings, seasonings and straight marinades. Even dry mix marinades, with olive oil and some added acidity (lemon juice, vinegar, wine) become flavourful tenderisers. And the wet mixes are invaluable as sauces or dressings in their own right to use before, during or after cooking.

Bombay Spice Mix

Mumbai (old Bombay) seems to me one of the world's most fascinating places, and the street foods there made my palate rejoice for months. Its foods present a feast of colours, textures, spiciness, sweetness and saltiness; but with a balance and earthiness. Asafoetida lends a curious pungent charm: it is optional but it integrates beautifully into the finished mix.

Makes about 125g

To buy/find

2 cinnamon sticks, crushed

2 tablespoons coriander seeds

1 tablespoon fenugreek seeds

15g dried crushed hot red chillies

1 tablespoon cloves

6–8 dried bay leaves, crumbled

50g coarse salt crystals

2 teaspoons asafoetida powder (optional)

1 tablespoon nigella or black cumin seeds

To prepare/cook Combine the first 6 ingredients in a *karai*, heavy iron pan or wok. Dry roast until aromatic, then cool. Using a large pestle and mortar or an electric spice grinder, grind these to a powder, adding the salt towards the end. Stir in the asafoetida powder and nigella seeds.

To present Present in a stoppered jar or pot. Use in spicy Indian dishes as a coating, a seasoning or a dry marinade.

'Ali Berberé' Mix

Said to be Ethiopian in origin, this dry spice mix, based upon one called Berberé, can be used to rub over meats, fish or chicken before cooking. *Wats*, which are famous African dishes, and also some North African *tajines* contain similar sorts of spicy coatings to impart colour, flavour and tenderness. Use this dry mix to spice up your barbecues, grills, chargrills and roasts.

Makes about 125g

To buy/find

2 tablespoons dried black peppercorns

2 tablespoons allspice berries

1 tablespoon whole cloves

2 tablespoons dried hot red chillies

5cm piece cinnamon, crumbled

1 tablespoon coriander seeds

1 nutmeg, grated

20 green cardamom pods, crushed

2 teaspoons turmeric powder

2 teaspoons dried ginger

To prepare/cook Put the peppercorns, allspice, cloves, chillies, cinnamon and coriander into a dry frying pan or *karai* or wok. Heat briefly, stirring, until they begin to smell aromatic. Do not let them darken and scorch or they will be bitter. Tip them out of the pan and cool them. Add the grated nutmeg, the cardamoms, the turmeric and ginger. Using a big mortar and pestle or an electric spice grinder, pound or grind the mixture to a coarse dry powder. Cool.

To present Store in jars and use at an *al fresco* meal as you like.

Mexicana Mix

Spice mixes are created in Mexican families and passed on like precious gifts. Use this mix to impart a taste of Mexico to any meal, and a warm gold colour – due to annatto, a pigment beloved by Mexican cooks; look for this in Spanish delis.

Makes about 100g

To buy/find

2 tablespoons allspice berries

1 teaspoon dried oregano

2 teaspoons annatto powder or 1 teaspoon saffron stigma

15g dried *chipotle* flesh (smoked, dried jalapeño), torn into tiny pieces

4 tablespoons mild or hot paprika

4 tablespoons *piloncillo* or soft dark brown sugar

1 tablespoon coarse salt crystals or kosher salt

1 teaspoon lemon pepper

To prepare/cook Combine the allspice, oregano, annatto powder and *chipotle* pieces in a dry pan and dry roast briefly over a gas flame or a barbecue. Do not let them scorch, merely become aromatic. Cool these. Put them, the paprika, half of the sugar, all of the salt and the lemon pepper into a mortar and pestle (in Mexico it's a basalt *molcahete* – perfect for this) or electric spice grinder and pound or grind to a gritty powder. Stir in the remaining sugar.

To present Store in a stoppered bottle or screw-top jar. Use as required.

Note:

Annatto powder is sometimes hard to find. You can use annatto seeds but you'll need an electric spice grinder to grind them really well. Begin by grinding them with the salt and paprika to give more bulk then dry roast the mixture with the allspice, oregano and chipotle. *Continue as instructed above.*

Harissa

In North Africa, harissa is a popular hot, red, spicy condiment. It is frequently served with couscous. Don't limit its use only to this, however: use it stirred into mayonnaise, soft cheese or yogurt or shake it up in vinaigrette. Eat it, also, on its own, as a seasoning. Take a little jar along with you on your next portable feast. It works wonders.

Makes 450ml

To buy/find

30g large, dried hot red chillies, crumbled

1 carrot, sliced

2 large red peppers, cored, deseeded, cubed

8 garlic cloves, crushed

1 teaspoon salt, or more to taste

2 tablespoons green cardamom pods to yield 1/2 teaspoon black seeds

2 tablespoons each of cumin and coriander seeds

1 tablespoon black peppercorns

75ml extra virgin olive oil

To prepare/cook Cover the chillies, carrot and red peppers in a medium saucepan, with about 5cm of boiling water. Bring pan contents back to boiling, cover, reduce to a lively simmer and cook for 15 minutes or until tender. Drain the solids. Put them into a food processor. In a mortar and pestle, pound the garlic, salt, black cardamom seeds (having discarded the seed pods), the cumin and coriander seeds and black peppercorns. Add to the food processor with 2/3 of the olive oil and process to a rough paste. Taste and add more salt if necessary. Pour the harissa into one medium, or several small, clean, ideally sterilised, jars, leaving 1cm headroom. Pour on the remaining olive oil as a seal. Refrigerate, once cooled, for up to 1 month, topping up the olive oil seal after each use.

To present Present in the container.

Peri Peri Wet Mix

Part Africa, part Portugal, this vinaigrette-type mix will enliven any meat, fish, chicken or game you use it with. It is also good with pasta or couscous – it adds powerful hotness, so use with care.

Makes about 150ml

To buy/find

2 tablespoons dried, or 4 tablespoons fresh red bird's eye chillies, half crumbled or chopped, half left whole

4 garlic cloves, chopped

shredded zest and juice of 2 limes

100ml peanut (groundnut) or corn oil

1 teaspoon sea salt flakes

To prepare/make Pierce the whole chillies with a pin. Shake up all the ingredients in a pretty, stoppered glass jar or flask, ideally with a non-metal lid. Use as a marinade, to baste, or as a salad dressing.

Provençal Wet Mix

The foods you eat in Les Alpilles and Les Baux de Provence in France have some of the most intense flavours ever. Sun and ancient soils, perhaps, and their traditional growing methods, no doubt contribute to it. I tasted a vinaigrette mix, very like this, one sunny Saturday. It's the lavender which is so haunting, and the hint of orange. But use it fresh to exploit the vivid tastes.

Makes about 150ml

To buy/find

2 teaspoons sea salt flakes

3 garlic cloves, crushed, but left whole

100ml first cold-pressed extra virgin olive oil

30ml red wine vinegar

2 stems (about 15cm total) fresh rosemary, bruised

8 fresh heads lavender, crumbled (or 1/2 teaspoon, dried)

7.5cm strip fresh orange zest, crushed

8 fresh basil leaves, torn or chopped

To prepare/make Pound the garlic and salt together using a pestle and mortar to make a paste. Combine this with the remaining ingredients in a large sealable glass jar or a flask with a cork stopper. Shake well. Leave in a warm place. Use within 1 day. Great for salads, for tenderising red meats and for use with roasted, cold chicken. Also useful for pouring over grilled goat's cheese in a salad.

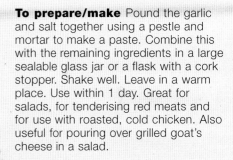

Picnic

Picnics rarely happen without a few bursts of delighted laughter. Appetites seem sharpened: any food tastes better out of doors for some mysterious, inexplicable reason. Perhaps it's the sense of adventure, the spur of improvisation. Will the sunshine last? Can we keep the Riesling chilled? Consider, too, that picnics can happen in the office, on trains and bikes. Picnicking can easily become a passion.

Bento picnic *page 74*

Orchard picnic *page 78*

Garden picnic *page 86*

Summer isn't really summer without a picnic. But picnics and portable feasts can be arranged, for many different situations, in the blink of an eye. This is much of the reason for their charm. Spontaneity can make the most simple picnic into a memorable one.

Portable food requires a bit of creativity and, at times, ingenuity. Invention often spells fun, so gaiety is often a natural outcome. Food tastes best when people feel relaxed so these ideas are ideal for enjoyable party giving. Fresh air whips up anticipation, too.

Sand in the sandwiches, caterpillars in the salad: these can spoil the happiest of occasions, however, so some tips about organisation are useful. Many are included here. On the other hand, iced soup sipped at the beach or strawberries, cream and meringues under the blossom trees can seem superb celebrations in themselves: really easy, simple ones.

Sashimi and chopsticks taken from a neat, pretty bento box, at your desk or in the park, is just one of the many ways to enliven your week.

Picnics are often successful because the young can run about, jump, play, hide, explore and come back, exhausted and hungry, to tuck into food with their fingers. Gourmet picnickers often use seasonal treats or regional specialities as a spur for their own feasts. Local breads, organically produced wines, unusual salad herbs, hand-made goat's cheeses and pick-your-own berries or stone fruits can be the basis for wonderful, epicurean meals *al fresco*.

In other words, picnicking can be anything and all that you need it to be. Picnics appeal to 8- and 80-year-olds alike.

Picnics often imply an element of surprise, of impromptu performance, even of risk. Rain might fall, the tablecloth may almost blow away; the Brie will be trickling out of its box: but boredom will certainly not be a bugbear. Huge appetites, laughter and true participation are much more likely. As long as some common sense has played its part and the food and drink are appropriate, not too ambitious nor too difficult to carry or to eat; as long as wine glasses remain unbroken, some peppercorns stay in the pepper grinder and the melon doesn't roll into the lake, there's a chance that the day will be a success. Especially if the air smells good.

My picnic ideas are traditional and also eclectic; elegant and also earthy; sometimes complex but more often very simple. A combination of home-made, shop-bought and communally-provided items can easily add up to a splendid feast: trust your instincts and the weather and go for it.

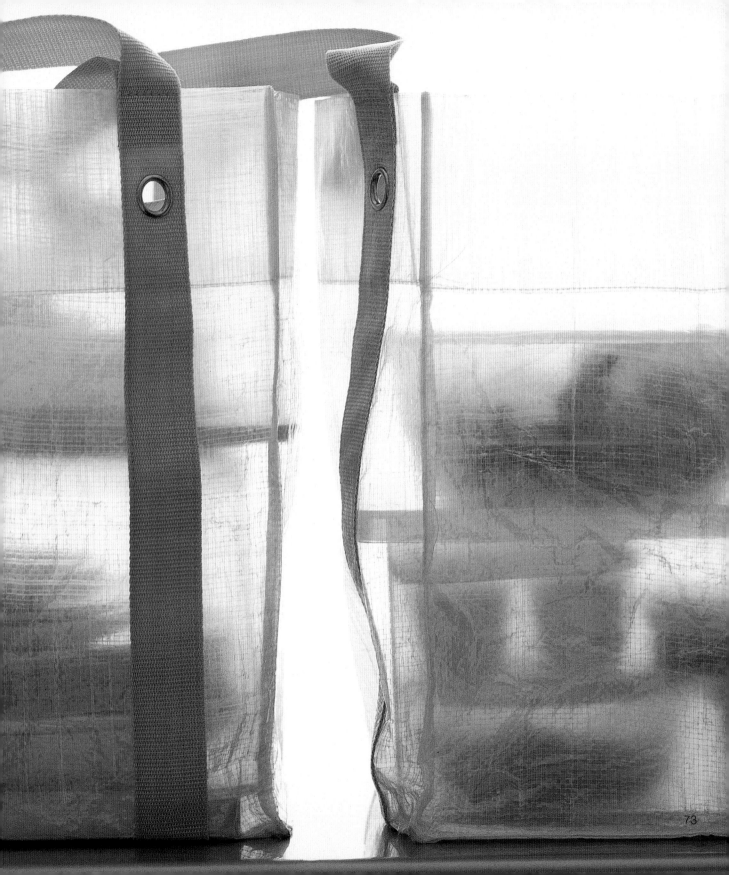

Sashimi of Salmon & Tuna

Always use sushi-grade, raw fish from a reputable source for this recipe. Alternatively substitute prepared smoked salmon in the piece, smoked eel or cooked prawn tails, if you prefer. Keep the fish very chilled. Pack it tightly into the box with no room for movement. Perilla leaves, green or purple, have an intense, almost medicinal flavour – they are traditionally enjoyed with sashimi. Japanese grocers often stock them, fresh, but nasturtium leaves are an alternative.

Serves 1

To buy/find

50g sushi grade raw salmon

50g raw belly tuna

4 fresh perilla leaves or nasturtium leaves (optional)

25g shredded white daikon radish, to garnish (optional)

1 small sachet/tube *wasabi* paste (green horseradish)

1 small sachet/pot pickled pink ginger

1 small bottle or pot of *shoyu* sauce (soy sauce)

green tea, to drink

tropical fruits e.g. mangosteen, lychees or rambutan

To prepare/make Holding the fish carefully on a clean surface, skin-side uppermost, use a cleaver or sharp knife to cut it cleanly into 1 x 2cm bite-sized pieces. Keep the fish in its original shape. If using the leaves, pack them into the appropriate section of the bento box or wrap them in waxed paper. Add the radish garnish either in its own section or else in waxed paper, as well. Pack the condiments, in their own containers, nearby.

To present Add the can or bottle of chilled green tea, wrapped in a napkin, and the washed, clean tropical fruits to the bento box. Seal well. Pack chopsticks and a china spoon. Secure it all tightly or tie well with its band, with ribbons or its ties.

Sticky Rice

Japanese sushi rice, stubby and plump, is correctly cooked after a brief soaking time, in very little extra liquid. Use Thai jasmine rice or even plain, simple old pudding rice if you prefer: less authentic but perfectly acceptable, but allow 200ml of water for these.

Serves 1

To buy/find

100g Japanese sushi rice

150ml boiling water

1 teaspoon finely sliced fresh root ginger

1 tablespoon mirin (sweetened rice wine)

1 tablespoon white rice vinegar or white wine vinegar

1/4 teaspoon salt (optional)

To prepare/cook Swish the rice around under running cold water until the water looks clear. Add more cold water. Leave for 30 minutes. Drain. In a medium saucepan, bring the rice and the measured volume of water back to boiling point. Cover with a lid, reduce the heat and cook for 15 minutes or until all the liquid is absorbed. Tip the rice out on to a plate. Leave uncovered for several minutes. Fan the rice to cool it and stir in the ginger, mirin, vinegar and salt. Chill it if it is likely to become warm in transit since rice is a non-acid food which can spoil in warm conditions.

To present Pack the rice loosely into an appropriate compartment in the box, separated from the fish and condiments.

Miso Soup

Traditionalists make fresh *dashi* stock from scratch using dried tuna and dried sea vegetables. It is delicious, very worth the effort, but if time is an issue substitute a good *dashi* packet mix from an Asian store, as many young Japanese cooks do.

Serves 1

To buy/find

85g dried *soba* or *udon* noodles, boiled, or 175g cooked, drained, chilled noodles

1 teaspoon dark red miso paste

1 garlic clove, thinly sliced

200ml hot *dashi* stock (see above)

1 spring onion, sliced into long, thin strips

1 sheet *nori* (dried seaweed), scissor-shredded, to serve

To prepare/cook Put the cooked noodles into a lidded bowl or appropriate container which fits well into the bento box. Stir the miso and garlic into the *dashi*. Add the spring onion. Pour this over the noodles. Cool. Chill in its container.

To present Pack the *nori* shreds, separately. Add the miso soup to the bento box just before it is secured.

Game plan for bento box

Transport your bento box, cool, to your location. Uncover, unpack and enjoy: dip the sashimi into *shoyu*, *wasabi* and ginger and eat.

Bento picnic

Japanese food, recently, has become much more mainstream and highly popular. The elegance and deliciousness of the packed bento-box meal makes it the perfect picnic concept. Take this picnic from your office into the park, enjoy it as a theatre supper or a celebration brunch. It has both style and content.

To eat
Sashimi of salmon and tuna
Sticky rice
Miso soup
Lychees and mangosteens
To drink
Green tea or spritzer or beer

Park picnic

This picnic menu is a beauty: enjoy it under the trees, amongst the roses or on lawns surrounded by statues. A Shiraz would complement the leg of lamb, which is taken to the picnic whole and carved to order. Let scented Muscat flatter the cheese. Hummus flatbreads and salad leaves precede the feast.

Garlic- & Anchovy-stuffed Roast Lamb

Gigot (in France and Scotland) or leg of lamb is a prime cut and splendid as picnic fare. Cook it, ready-seasoned as in this recipe, with anchovy and garlic and it becomes a perfect portable feast: neither redcurrant jelly nor mint sauce will be needed. It tastes brilliant hot, warm or cold, and is an epicurean dish. The roasted onions which accompany it are also superb.

Serves 8

To buy/find

1 leg spring lamb, about 2.5–2.75kg

100g canned anchovy fillets, drained and halved

10 garlic cloves, halved lengthwise

20 pistachios, skinned and blanched

2 tablespoons extra virgin olive oil

freshly ground salt and black pepper

4 red onions, unpeeled, halved crosswise

3 tablespoons aged balsamic vinegar

120ml robust red wine

To prepare/cook Pat the lamb all over with kitchen paper to dry. Roll up an anchovy fillet half around each garlic half and each pistachio. Using a small sharp knife make a series of 2cm deep small incisions in the fleshiest parts of the lamb. Leaving the blade still in the incision, twist it and insert the anchovy roll. Do this all over the upper part of the leg at intervals until it is studded with these aromatics. Place in a large roasting pan. Drizzle the olive oil all over the lamb and sprinkle with salt and pepper. Roast the lamb in an oven preheated to 190°C for 20 minutes per 500g and 20 minutes over: 2–2¼ hours. Estimate roughly 45 minutes before the end of cooking time: add the onions, cut sides up, all round the roast. Take out the lamb when it is cooked and transfer it and the onions to a portable serving dish. Drizzle the balsamic vinegar over the onions. Leave the meat and its juices to 'set'. Now pour off excessive fat from the roasting pan and leave the 'jus': stir in the wine. Cook, over moderate heat, stirring to dissolve the sediment until you have a rich thick red wine sauce. Pour it into a sealable container and pack it with the lamb and onions.

To present Carve the meat thickly on site, adding a share of onions and the unthickened red wine sauce.

To eat
Hummus *page 22* with flatbreads and salad leaves
Garlic- and anchovy-stuffed roast lamb
Muscat and *Banon* goat's cheese
To drink
Shiraz

Orchard picnic

A five-course picnic which could be fun to serve in an orchard or back garden. Bring the soup out, hot, from the kitchen. Have the tart, chicken and salad ready and waiting. Let the pashka puddings be turned out on the spot if you like. Offer frozen vodka with beer chasers to start: end with rum-scented tea.

Field Mushroom Tart

This earthy mushroom tart is intensely flavourful. Do not be tempted to substitute button mushrooms: use big, dark 'flats'. Sliced porcini (ceps) would be the only other alternative: fresh or from jars.

Serves 8

To buy/find

4 large, flat field or portobello-type mushrooms

50g garlic and parsley butter

2 tablespoons extra virgin olive oil

150ml single cream

3 free range eggs, beaten

375g short pastry, rolled 3mm thick

1 slice stale bread, processed or grated into crumbs

small bunch of chives, parsley, oregano or a mixture, chopped

To prepare/cook Remove the stalks from the mushrooms; trim the stalks and slice them thinly. Wipe the mushrooms using a damp cloth but do not wash. Heat the flavoured butter and the oil in a large, non-stick frying pan. Add the mushrooms, gill-side downwards, and the sliced stalks. Cook 5 minutes, uncovered. Turn them over, cook, covered, for another 5 minutes. Preheat the oven to 220°C. Using a fork lightly beat the cream and eggs.

Use the pastry to line a 25cm fluted, loose-bottomed flan tin, pressing it into the tin. Trim the edges and discard the trimmings. Halve each mushroom cap crosswise and put in the pastry case, gills up, in a decorative pattern; add the sliced stalks. Pour the egg mixture around the mushrooms. Stir the crumbs into the frying pan to soak up any remaining butter-oil mix. Scatter these over the flan. Bake towards the top of the oven for about 20 minutes then reduce heat to 180°C. Cook for a further 15–20 minutes or until the egg is set firm.

To present Scatter the fresh herbs over the top. Serve in slices or wedges, hot, warm or cool.

Italianate Chicken Breasts

This easy recipe tastes good, transports well and is perfect finger food. Because of the flavourful Italian ingredients it needs no seasoning whatsoever.

Serves 8

To buy/find

8 boneless, skinless chicken breasts

150g mozzarella, sliced into 16

100g pecorino or scamorza cheese, sliced into 16

8 sprigs rosemary or fresh basil, halved

16 slices garlicky salami, e.g. Milano

8 slices prosciutto di Parma (cured Italian ham)

8 garlic cloves, crushed

4 tablespoons extra virgin olive oil

fresh flatleaf parsley, to garnish

To prepare/cook Make two crosswise cuts, three-quarters of the way through each chicken breast, at a slight angle. Push first a slice of mozzarella, then pecorino, then a herb sprig into each slash. Remove any skin from the salami, fold each slice in two, and push one into each cut as well. Continue until each chicken breast cut is evenly filled and all ingredients are used up. Slide a ham slice under each chicken breast, and push a garlic clove between the ham and chicken. Loosely wrap the ham over the chicken. Set the ham-wrapped chicken breasts on a folded sheet of aluminium foil on an oven tray. Drizzle 1 1/2 teaspoons of oil over each and fold the foil to enclose. Bake in an oven preheated to 200°C for 20–25 minutes or until cooked through. Refold the foil to enclose and wrap the chicken for transport.

To present Serve hot, warm or cool, just as they are, removed from the foil.

To eat
Hot borscht and rolls *page 34*
Field mushroom tart
Italianate chicken breasts
Green salad *page 94*
Pashka *page 106*
To drink
Frozen vodka *page 117*
Iced beer chasers
Scented tea with rum *page 118*

Harvest picnic

Stuffed Quail

The only thing better on a picnic than a stuffed quail is a boneless stuffed quail. Almost every bit can be eaten and it is blissfully easy to manage. Look out for these in top-class game dealers, butchers and delis. Alternatively, opt for a variety of superb salami.

Serves 4

To buy/find

8 prepared quail or boneless quail

85g seedless muscat raisins

8 slices prosciutto di Parma (cured Italian ham)

50g toasted pinenuts

8–16 vine leaves, fresh, or preserved, blanched and drained

1–2 tablespoons extra virgin olive oil

6 tablespoons muscat-type wine

To prepare/cook Choose a large, shallow flameproof casserole or a metal baking pan into which the quail fit snugly. Mix the raisins, half the ham, scissor-chopped, and the pinenuts together. Push some of this stuffing loosely inside the cavity of each bird. Wrap a slice of prosciutto loosely around each bird. Set each wrapped bird inside a nest of vine leaves in the casserole or baking pan. Rub or dot each bird with a little oil or bacon fat. Splash the wine over. Bake the birds, uncovered, in an oven preheated at 180°C for 35–45 minutes or until rosy and lightly golden, cooked well through and aromatic.

(Alternatively cook them hot and fast: 220°C for 20–25 minutes and serve them far more rare.)

To serve Take the whole casserole to the picnic, wrapped first in foil then in a heavy cloth. Serve hot, warm or cool.

This stylish outdoor menu starts with radishes eaten with butter and salt, French style, and ends with Roquefort and grapes, the same way. In between the offerings become Italianate: quails or charcuterie (*salumi*) and saffron risotto. A Côtes du Rhône would suit such food. Hot coffee and Calvados end the meal.

Saffron Risotto

Classic Milanese risotto uses Italian *superfino* rice such as Arborio: stubby, creamy grains which hold together. Buy it from a reputable deli or good grocer. Although it's usual to add the stock slowly, stirring all the while, you can add it all at once, part-cover the risotto and cook for 20–25 minutes, with an occasional stir. It's up to you.

Serves 4

To buy/find

1.75 litres chicken stock

1/4 teaspoon powered saffron or 2 pinches saffron stigma

85g butter

4 tablespoons extra virgin olive oil

1 onion, sliced

350g risotto rice

1 teaspoon sea salt flakes

freshly ground black pepper

75g Parmesan cheese, in the piece

To prepare/cook Heat the stock in a large pan, and add the saffron, stirring it in well until it dissolves and gilds the stock. Heat half of the butter and all of the oil together in a large, heavy-based, frying pan, add the onion and let it soften. Now stir in the rice and allow it to be well coated. Add the stock, a ladleful (about 350ml or so) at a time, stirring, and leave to cook gently until all the stock has been absorbed. Repeat this process about 4 more times over the 25–28 minutes it takes. (Alternatively add all the stock at once, stir, bring to bubbling, reduce heat to slow, simmer, covered, for 20–25 minutes, stirring now and then.) By the end it should be soft, soupy but creamy. Add the reserved butter and the salt and pepper. Spoon the risotto into a lidded casserole.

To present Take the Parmesan in the piece. Serve the risotto from its dish – it's delicious hot, warm or cool. Add curls of cheese to taste on site, using a potato peeler or sharp knife.

Romantic picnic

Seductive food is often simple, sensual and tactile: contrasts are stimulating, too. Here, hot, spicy tiny sausages are alternated with a cold, briny oyster. Use fingers. Pass the chilled Champagne. Next, enjoy noodles with a truffle dressing: superb. Rocket and Parmesan provide pungency, stimulus.

Iced Rock Oysters with Spicy Chipolatas

In Bordeaux fresh oysters are often served followed by freshly cooked hot sausages. Spicy merguez are another alternative; here is a version using spicy chipolatas. The idea is: pop an icy oyster into your mouth followed by a peppery hot sausage. The oyster shells can go into the sea, the sand or the pebbles – perfectly biodegradable – or you can dig them into your garden.

Serves 2

To buy/find

350g skinless pork chipolata sausages

2 tablespoons cracked black pepper

1 tablespoon finely chopped garlic

3 kaffir lime leaves, scissor shredded

2 tablespoons soy sauce

1 tablespoon olive oil

12 fresh, live rock oysters

1 lemon or lime, halved

To prepare/cook Halve the chipolatas to make cocktail size sausages. Mix together the pepper, garlic and kaffir lime shreds. Roll the chipolatas in the soy sauce, and then in the garlic mix. Heat the olive oil in a non-stick frying pan and cook the sausages for 5–6 minutes or until firm and golden brown all over. Pack in foil, then wrap in cloth to keep hot. Open the oysters and set them, deep shell downwards in a container lined with crushed ice. Set the top shells back on the oysters. Pack a clean cloth on top to keep the oysters in position.

To present Unwrap and serve the oysters with the chipolatas, and lemon or lime for squeezing. Eat an oyster, then a spicy hot sausage.

Tagliatelle
with Truffle Butter

This tagliatelle has a touch of luxury. It is cooked in flavourful broth then dressed with some truffles. It can be eaten hot, warm or cold – but do not chill. Truffles, black or white, are a seasonal delicacy: neither cheap nor easy to locate, though they are well worth finding. Look for clean, dense truffles, aromatic and undamaged. Even a 15g specimen would be sufficient for this dish. Alternatively use whole canned or bottled truffles.

Serves 2

To buy/find

200g dried tagliatelle pasta

750ml chicken or veal stock, heated to boiling

2 garlic cloves, crushed

salt and freshly ground black pepper

2 tablespoons extra virgin olive oil

25g butter

15–25g fresh white or black truffle, finely shaved or shredded or canned or bottled whole truffles, drained

2 squeezes lemon juice

fresh chives, finely or coarsely snipped

To prepare/cook Cook the pasta in the boiling stock until *al dente*: drain. In the same hot pan, heat the garlic, salt and pepper with the oil, butter and half the truffle. Add a squeeze of lemon. Put the cooked pasta into the pan and toss it carefully to coat. Transfer to a portable container and dot the remaining truffle over the pasta, scattering the chives on top and adding another squeeze of lemon.

To present Serve in individual bowls.

To eat
Iced rock oysters with spicy chipolatas
Tagliatelle with truffle butter
Rocket and Parmesan salad *page 94*
Fresh raspberries
To drink
Chilled Champagne

Bicycle picnic

A bit of a surprise treat, this menu, with perfect lean fillet of beef in thick slices and old-fashioned baked potatoes: select a topping and add some herbs on site. Drink some fresh spring water and take a bottle of Beaujolais to share – crisp apples, some bitter chocolate and Brazil nuts complete the menu.

To eat
Baked spiced beef
Herbed potatoes
Apples, bitter chocolate and Brazil nuts
To drink
Beaujolais
Mineral water

Baked Spiced Beef

Cold roast beef fillet, rubbed with spices, and surrounded by its own jellied juices: how easy, how superb. Great food for any occasion – any location.

Serves 8

To buy/find

1kg beef fillet, in the piece
2 teaspoons allspice berries
1 tablespoon black peppercorns
1 teaspoon cloves
1/2 teaspoon ground mace
2 teaspoons coarse salt crystals
2 garlic cloves, crushed to a paste
1 tablespoon vinaigrette
2 tablespoons virgin olive oil

To prepare/cook Tie the beef fillet in four places, crosswise, with string so that it cooks in a good shape, pushing a metal skewer through it, lengthwise, for the same reason. Using a pestle and mortar, or an electric spice grinder, pound or grind the allspice, peppercorns, cloves, mace and salt to a dryish powder. Mix the garlic paste and vinaigrette together. Place the beef in a metal roasting pan, and rub the garlic mixture over. Pat on the allspice mixture. Leave to stand 20 minutes or up to 1 hour at room temperature. Preheat the oven to 230°C. Heat the oil in a large non-stick frying pan and brown the meat for about 8 minutes, turning to cook all four sides. Roast the beef for 13 minutes per 500g (26 minutes, no extra). If using a meat thermometer, the internal temperature must be 65°C for rare, 70°C for medium rare. The beef should be crusty outside, rosy inside. Leave the meat to stand in its roasting pan for at least 20 minutes to rest. Remove the metal skewer. If you must, refrigerate the beef, but it tastes better cool, not chilled.

To present Transport the beef whole or carved: serve in 1cm slices, hot, warm or cool, with any accompanying pan juices. (If cooked, cooled and refrigerated the day before, these juices may well have jellied.) Serve absolutely plain or with some horseradish sauce and coarse grain mustard.

Herbed Potatoes

Here's an idea for nicely portable baked potatoes: good for active adventurers to take on their journeys – classic but always sustaining and delicious. Add toppings according to what pleases you.

Serves 8

To buy/find

8 baking potatoes, washed and dried
120g garlic or herb butter
salt and freshly ground black pepper

Topping alternatives:
200ml pot natural yogurt
or 100g grated Cheddar cheese
or 100g sun-dried tomato paste
or 100g hummus or guacamole
or 100g sauce tartare
handful fresh herbs e.g. parsley, chives, basil, tarragon

To prepare/cook Push a long metal skewer through four potatoes; repeat with the other four. Set them directly on to the top rack of an oven preheated to 220°C. Bake for 11/4–11/2 hours or until soft when pressed. Remove the potatoes from the oven and remove the skewer. Make a criss-cross cut on the flat top of each hot potato. Squeeze slightly to open them, and insert about a tablespoon of garlic or herb butter; sprinkle with some salt and pepper. Press on the cuts to close them. Wrap each hot potato first in foil, then kitchen paper, then foil again. This way they'll stay hot for some hours, and undamaged. Take a selection of topping alternatives in sturdy pots with lids. Wrap the herbs in wetted paper, then foil and take along too.

To present Unwrap the potatoes. Squeeze open. Dot on some topping, add fresh herbs and eat.

Garden picnic

This selection of charming, child-friendly recipes adds up to a good finger-food picnic for children of all ages and adults young at heart, too. Home-made lemonade with soda and mildly fizzy ginger beer provide pleasant drinks. There's also a do-it-yourself dessert.

Chicken & Parsley Salad

A simple, child-friendly salad which is plain and easy, yet surprisingly sophisticated for all its simplicity. A 1kg roast chicken easily provides 600g chicken strips.

Serves 6

To buy/find

600g cooked chicken, skinless, boneless, in strips

2 tablespoons milk

4 tablespoons mayonnaise

2 tablespoons chopped parsley

salt and freshly ground white pepper

2 Romaine (Cos) lettuce hearts

1 container salad cress

To prepare Place the chicken in a portable container. Whisk together the milk, mayonnaise, parsley and salt and pepper. Drizzle this over the chicken. Cover. Seal well. Pack the washed, still-wet lettuce hearts separately.

To present Pull apart the lettuce. Lay the leaves in a neat row, parallel. Spoon a little chicken into each leaf. Snip or pinch off the salad cress and sprinkle on top. Eat in your fingers.

Tortilla Omelette

This is one of the world's most loved, most delicious and most portable of dishes but there are one or two authentic tricks to learn to make sure it emerges perfectly. If you want to cook individual tortillas, sauté the vegetables in a large pan and cook the egg and vegetable mixture in small cast-iron frying pans, about 12.5cm in diameter – these will cook more quickly than a large tortilla.

Makes 6

To buy/find

7 tablespoons extra virgin olive oil

500g large potatoes, peeled, quartered and thickly sliced

450g (about 2) Spanish onions, thickly sliced

2 red peppers, cored, deseeded and diced

8 large fresh free-range eggs

1 teaspoon salt

1/2 teaspoon freshly ground black pepper

To prepare/cook Heat 4 tablespoons of the oil in a large heavy grill-safe frying pan about 30cm in diameter and add the prepared potatoes, onion and red peppers. Sauté over moderate heat for about 15 minutes, stirring occasionally. Cover the pan and cook for a further 15 minutes or until tender. Using a fork, lightly beat the eggs, salt and pepper in a large bowl. Tip the potato mixture into the beaten eggs. Quickly wash and dry the frying pan and return to the heat, adding the remaining olive oil. When the oil is hot, pour the egg and potato mixture into the frying pan. Cook over high heat for 3–4 minutes, then reduce heat to moderate. Cook the tortilla, undisturbed, for 10–12 minutes until the base is golden and firm. With a fork, pull back the edges of the tortilla and allow the uncooked mixture to run underneath. Preheat the grill and cook the top of the tortilla for 2–3 minutes or until it sets firm.

To present Take the tortilla in its pan, divide into wedges and serve.

Note:

Both Fauchon and Hédiard, in Paris, have sold the small cast-iron pans for years, or they are available from specialist kitchen suppliers.

To eat
Ham and gherkin roll-ups *page 42*
Chicken and parsley salad
Tortilla omelette
Watercress sandwiches *page 43*
Bananas, honey and cream
To drink
Lemonade and soda, and ginger beer *page 122*

Salads & vegetables

Little seems more refreshing and welcome, in the course of a portable feast, than some simple, crisp, crunchy salad leaves with a trickle of good dressing: a plateful of glorious greens. Some vividly ripe tomatoes or waxy baby potatoes can be utterly satisfying, too. Such treats could comprise the bulk of the meal. Especially if there's good bread, cheese and fruit to follow.

Bacon, Rocket & Leek Salad *page 92*

Salad dressings *page 98*

Rice Noodle Salad *page 101*

Salads for portable feasts and picnics should be based on the fresh leafy salads, crisp vegetables and fragrant herbs that are in season; on the grains, beans, root vegetables, pasta and rice that are available; and on what can be bought en route. The ideal is vivid freshness, jewel colours, clear, bright flavours.

Dressings are best made and packed separately and added at time of serving, although some salads improve with being dressed ahead of time, such as wild rice salads, bean salads and pasta salads.

To keep salad greens fresh they need to be wetted. Well-dampened newspaper will do; so will snap-top plastic boxes, plastic bags with a few ice cubes tucked into the base and even a plastic salad-spinner, top, base and all, if you add a splash of iced water before leaving or a few ice cubes.

Some salad stuffs: endive, chicory, fennel bulbs, celery heads, whole cucumber, tomatoes, Cos lettuces and baby Gem-type lettuces are all robust enough to go as purchased and be torn or divided on the spot: participation is a good idea and fun for those unused to such activities. Don't forget a head of juicy garlic: it can bring a salad to life in seconds. Crush, chop or rub it around the salad bowl or rub it generously all over a slice of French bread and toss this deep in amongst the salad. I like to drizzle some olive oil and salt on to my bread as well. Share this out at the end, it is delicious. Take oil bottles and pepper and salt grinders on every portable feast.

Dressings for salads can as simple as you like: a scattering of herbs, crispy bacon bits or croûtons, a drizzle of extra virgin olive oil. Many of my recipes here include dressings. But if you take garlic, a lemon, oil and seasonings, you ensure that any salad will have a dressing made to order.

Go for lovely oils: I'd suggest a bottle or stoppered jug of estate-bottled, first, cold-pressed extra virgin olive oil as one of the most desirable. For Asian dishes, grapeseed or safflower oils are good choices. Sesame oil, chilli oil, truffle oil, hazelnut, pumpkin seed or walnut oils are all welcome additions, but go easy: these become oppressive if over-used. I usually mix them in the proportion of 4 parts of mild oil to 1 part flavoured oil.

As for the acid factor: lemons, limes or oranges, halved and squeezed on the spot, are a great bonus. Plain and flavoured vinegars from fruit vinegars to wine or cider types can all add interest. Rice vinegars can also be appropriate. Balsamic vinegar is to be treasured, used sparingly for great effect.

Nuts and seeds can add texture to a vinaigrette (my rule is 1 part acid, 4 or 5 parts good olive oil) and mustard will help emulsify it. Salts and peppers come in many forms. Select whatever suits you. I prefer flaky Maldon salt for its mellowness and the pleasure of crushing it in your fingers.

Pickled or dry salt-cured olives, green and black, can add appeal. Peppers, porcini mushrooms and chillies can all boost a salad, especially one based on pasta, rice, beans or couscous.

But remember: starchy foods and dressings should stay chilled to keep them safe for eating. Heat can cause spoilage. Take precautions to keep them cool, then relax and enjoy your *al fresco* meal.

Bacon, Rocket & Leek Salad

Bacon, leeks, fruit vinegar combined with the bitterness of rocket (arugula) make this salad a tonic in its own right.

Serves 4

To buy/find

2 medium leeks or 12 spring onions

3 tablespoons extra virgin olive oil

8 rashers smoked streaky bacon, rind trimmed, chopped

2 tablespoons raspberry or other fruit vinegar

100g (2 large handfuls) fresh rocket (arugula)

To prepare/cook Finely slice the white parts of the leek or spring onions crosswise into rings. Put into a sieve or colander. Slice the green sections into 5cm lengths, rinse well to clean them then slice them lengthwise into slim julienne strips. Put these into a saucepan. Boil a kettle of water and pour over the green leek or spring onion shreds. Bring the pan contents back to boiling point until the leeks turn a brilliant emerald green. Pour pan contents over the shredded white parts. Refresh leeks under cold water. Shake fairly dry. Pack into a salad bowl or a snap-top plastic box. Heat the olive oil in a frying pan and cook the bacon until crisp. Remove it from the pan using a slotted spoon. Allow it to cool and wrap it in foil. Now pour the vinegar into the drippings left in the pan and stir to make a dressing. Pour this into a screw-top jar, flask or bottle. Do not chill. Pack the wetted rocket (arugula) on top of the leek. Seal with plastic wrap if using a bowl, or close the lid of the box.

To present Toss the leek, bacon and dressing with the rocket (arugula) and serve.

Radicchio

with Red Onion Salad

This is a pretty celebration of colours, tastes and textures. If you use aged balsamic vinegar, reduce the amount, since it's far more intense.

Serves 4

To buy/find

2–3 heads radicchio (round, red Italian chicory)

2 red onions, thinly sliced

100g raw broad beans (optional)

4 tablespoons extra virgin olive oil

2 tablespoons hazelnut oil

2 garlic cloves, crushed

3 tablespoons balsamic vinegar (or 1 if aged)

squeeze of lemon juice (optional)

75g salted, roast hazelnuts, coarsely chopped

sea salt flakes and freshly ground black pepper

To prepare/make Separate the washed radicchio heads but keep the cup shapes intact. Put the onions into a sieve. Pour some boiling water over them to blanch them then refresh immediately in cold water. Drain. Pack these in a salad bowl, snap-top box or salad spinner. Wrap the broad beans in a twist of waxed paper and pack with the salad. Combine the oils, garlic, vinegar, lemon juice, nuts and seasoning. Whisk or shake to blend. Take the dressing in a screw-top jar, flask or stoppered bottle.

To present Using salad servers, toss all the components together with the dressing. Serve without too much delay.

Rocket & Parmesan Salad

This salad takes seconds to prepare, and combines the lively taste of rocket (arugula) with the robust flavour of the best Parmesan.

Serves 4

To buy/find

350g bunch of fresh rocket (arugula)

small bottle estate-bottled cold, first-pressed olive oil

250g Parmesan cheese (Parmigiano Reggiano)

To prepare/make Take the rocket (arugula) washed, not shaken dry, packed in plastic or a waxed paper bag or a snap-top bowl. Take the little bottle of estate-bottled olive oil. Pack the Parmesan cheese and a potato peeler or sharp knife to cut it in curls or slivers.

To present When ready to eat, toss the rocket (arugula) with the olive oil and add the curls of cheese last.

Green Salad

Always look for the freshest, crispest and most flavourful salad stuffs. Take whole heads of washed salad and pull them apart at your feasting place. Pack herbs still in their bunches, washed, and cut or tear these at serving time. Take the vinaigrette (see page 98) or the dressing of your choice. Even a lemon, a little jar of virgin olive oil and some salt provide a dressing fit for a gourmet.

Serves 4

To buy/find

1 Romaine (Cos) heart, washed

1 Little Gem lettuce or Belgian endive, washed

2 handfuls bitter or peppery salad leaves such as watercress, rocket, escarole, batavia, frisée or red chard

1 small handful or bunch of fresh parsley, chives, mint, chervil or tarragon

1 red onion, finely sliced

To make/present Pack the whole salad heads in a snap-top box or salad spinner or wrap in wetted newspaper and put into a big plastic bag. Wrap the wetted leaves, the herb bunch and the sliced red onion, in its original form, in a similar bundle and seal. Take the dressing in a screw-top jar or take the ingredients and combine them on site. Unwrap, tear and combine the greens. Serve the green salad with your chosen dressing drizzled over.

Shredded Cos Salad

This is a lively salad with a sweetish, protein-rich dressing. It is unusual and interesting.

Serves 8

To buy/find

2 crisp Romaine (Cos) lettuces

Dressing:

2 tablespoons Dijon mustard

1 tablespoon clear honey

4 tablespoons natural yogurt

6 tablespoons extra virgin olive oil

1/2 teaspoon salt

2 teaspoons blue poppy seeds

2 tablespoons cider, tarragon or white wine vinegar

To make/prepare Wash the lettuces but don't shake them dry. Wrap in waxed paper or plastic or pack in a snap-top salad bowl. Mix the 7 dressing ingredients, in brief bursts, in a blender. If it seems too thick, add a little iced water. Blend again. Pour into a stoppered bottle, flask or screw-top jar. On site, pull off and pile up 8–10 of the outer, greener lettuce leaves from each lettuce. Roll them up. Cross-slice these leaves finely into shreds: a chiffonade. Pull off the remaining inner, paler leaves. Leave these whole.

To present When ready to eat, shake the dressing well, drizzle over the shreds of lettuce and toss together. Arrange the whole leaves round the edge of the bowl.

Potato & Cheese Salad

Easy, versatile, delicious: this salad can be served warm or cold made using whichever potatoes you choose. Some lively green leaves are added, as an edible garnish, at serving time.

Serves 8

To buy/find

900g smallish potatoes, scrubbed

salt

2 garlic cloves, crushed

200g soft blue cheese, such as Dolcelatte or Bleu de Bresse, cubed

100g fromage frais

4 tablespoons extra virgin olive oil

2 tablespoons tarragon vinegar

crushed black peppercorns (optional)

handful salad leaves, e.g. red chard, nasturtium, spinach, dandelion or frisée, to garnish

To prepare/make Place the potatoes in a pan and barely cover with boiling water; add salt to taste. Cook, covered, for 16–20 minutes or until tender but still firm. Drain them well. Turn off the heat and return them to the empty, dry pan. Cover the pan with a cloth and leave them for several minutes to dry out. Meanwhile make the dressing: put the garlic, blue cheese, fromage frais, oil and vinegar into a blender or food processor. Blend or process to a creamy dressing, adding a splash of cold water if the consistency is too thick. Cut the cooled potatoes into halves or quarters. Pack them into a portable container or clip-top bowl; sprinkle with some pepper, if you like. Pour the dressing over the top and seal the container. Take the washed salad leaves separately in a sealed container.

To present Mix the dressing in well or leave it as a topping. Toss the salad leaves on top. Serve the salad warm, or cool but not chilled.

Salad dressings

Salads can exist without dressings but good dressings add undoubted allure. Sometimes the dressing itself tastes so good alone that it dominates the entire meal: *salsa verde* and mayonnaise, for example. Others, with an Asian feel, can add subtle freshness and charm. Vinaigrette, that classic with its many potential variations, must also be rated one of the most useful of recipes.

Vinaigrette

The classic recipe is one part acid to five parts oil. Vary this according to your own needs and the occasion, using aromatics, spices and herbs as appropriate

Makes about 240ml

To buy/find

2 teaspoons English or Dijon mustard

2 tablespoons wine vinegar or lemon juice

8–12 tablespoons extra virgin olive oil

sea salt flakes and ground black pepper

To make Shake or whisk the ingredients together using a screw-top jar, a stoppered flask, a shaker or a bowl.

To present Transfer to an appropriate container as necessary.

Variations

Use grainy mustard. Add any of the following:

2 crushed garlic cloves;

crumbled dried chilli;

1 teaspoon clear honey;

chopped green herbs such as parsley, tarragon, chives, rosemary.

Mayonnaise

A classic but one which is made using a food processor; the texture is slightly more dense but this is lightened by the addition of boiling water.

Makes 450–500ml

To buy/find

1 egg, at room temperature

2 egg yolks, at room temperature

2 teaspoons Dijon mustard

1 tablespoon wine vinegar

1/2 teaspoon salt

1/4 teaspoon freshly ground black pepper

200ml extra virgin olive oil

200ml grapeseed oil

2 tablespoons boiling water

To make Combine the first 6 ingredients in a food processor. Process in a brief burst to mix. Mix the oils together, and, using a measuring jug, drizzle in the oils with the motor running. Gradually increase the trickle to a slow, steady pour until the mayonnaise thickens to a dense emulsion. Stop the machine now and then to scrape down the mixture from the sides. Add the boiling water in a slow drizzle. Transfer the finished mayonnaise to an airtight container. Cool. Refrigerate for up to 1 week.

To present Spoon out into a bowl or portable container. Keep cool and use the same day. It tastes best eaten at room temperature.

Variations

Aioli

Add 4 crushed chopped garlic cloves to the first lot of ingredients.

Seafood Mayonnaise

Add 2 tablespoons of tomato passata, 1/4 teaspoon anchovy sauce or paste and several shakes of Tabasco sauce to the mix before adding boiling water.

Note:

As this mayonnaise contains raw egg, do not serve to young children, or to anyone who is sick, elderly or pregnant.

Salsa Verde

A pungent, delicious green sauce with an Italianate touch. Combine the ingredients using a pestle and mortar and pound together or process briefly in a food processor in short bursts. Retain a chunky texture and clear colour if possible. The crumbs are entirely optional.

Makes about 400ml

To buy/find

50g tiny pickled capers, drained

50g canned or salted anchovies, chopped

50g small pickled gherkins (cornichons), chopped

1 tablespoon gherkin pickling liquid

4 garlic cloves, crushed and chopped

2 teaspoons pickled or dried green peppercorns, crushed

juice of 1 lemon (3 tablespoons)

1/2 teaspoon finely shredded lemon zest (optional)

1 handful fresh basil, parsley, lovage, oregano or marjoram, chopped

6–8 tablespoons extra virgin olive oil

2 tablespoons fresh breadcrumbs

To make Combine the first 6 ingredients in a mortar or food processor. Pound using a pestle or process briefly in bursts to mash and amalgamate the ingredients. Add the remaining ingredients, stirring to mix. Refrigerate and serve within 2 days.

To present Serve at room temperature as a sauce for chicken, fish, grills etc.

Nuoc Cham

Light, sharp but aromatic, thin dipping sauces such as this are common in Vietnam and are becoming popular world-wide. They can be used to pour over or as a dip. Make this sauce ahead or make it up on the spot from assembled ingredients. Good with noodles, rice, spring rolls, rice paper wraps, grills and leafy salads.

Makes 125ml

To buy/find

4 tablespoons rice vinegar or fresh lime juice

2 teaspoons clear honey or palm sugar

4 tablespoons chicken or vegetable stock

1 teaspoon dark sesame oil, or more to taste

2 tablespoons fish sauce

1–2 fresh birds' eye chillies, sliced

1–2 teaspoons toasted sesame seeds (optional)

To make Stir or shake together all the ingredients in a non-reactive bowl, screw-topped jar or stoppered flask until the honey or sugar is fully dissolved. Refrigerate for up to 1 week.

To present Shake again; serve cool or chilled in tiny, individual dishes or a bowl with a ladle.

Variations

Add 1 kaffir lime leaf, sliced in hair-like shreds.

Add 2 tablespoons chopped Vietnamese mint, Chinese chives or Thai holy basil.

Omit the sesame seeds and substitute finely chopped salted, roasted peanuts.

Wild Rice Salad

Dark, slim, wild rice (actually a type of wild aquatic grass seed) needs considerable cooking time; it has a nutty flavour and interesting texture. Cook it and dress it while it is hot: this way it absorbs all the flavours well.

Serves 3–4

To buy/find

250g wild rice, pre-soaked 2 hours if wished

750ml boiling salted water

4 garlic cloves, crushed then chopped

120ml virgin olive oil vinaigrette

1 bunch spring onions, shredded

1 handful mâche (lamb's lettuce), dandelion greens or watercress

30g fresh herbs, e.g. parsley, mint, basil, chives, chervil or a mixture

To prepare/cook Drain the pre-soaked rice or rinse it briefly in cold water. Cover it with the measured boiling salted water. Bring back to a boil, reduce the heat, part-cover and cook for 45–55 minutes or according to the packet instructions. The grains should have 'give' when pressed and some may have 'butterflied' into a double-curve shape. Drain the cooked rice. Combine the garlic and the vinaigrette. Stir this well into the rice. Cool slightly. Pack into a snap-top bowl, or use a bowl and cover tightly with plastic wrap. Put the prepared spring onions and salad greens of your choice and the herbs into another snap-top bowl or an airtight container such as a plastic bag. If using a bag, puff it up, full of air until it is tight, then secure with an elastic band: this keeps the succulent-textured greens crisp.

To present Toss everything together, leaving some of the herbs on top as garnish. Serve.

Variation

Add 4 hard-boiled eggs, shelled and halved lengthwise, to top this salad and make it into a full main dish, which can be served on its own. Follow it with crusty rolls, some superb raw fruit and some Brie or Camembert for a perfect, easy portable feast.

Rice Noodle Salad

A fresh, flavourful salad with both Thai and Vietnamese influences. Add the separately-cooked rare beef for avid omnivores and use fish sauce, but leave the salad free of meat and use light soy sauce for vegetarians: this salad works splendidly well both ways.

Serves 8

To buy/find

250g dried wide rice noodles

1/2 cucumber, in julienne strips

1 mango, in 1cm cubes or strips

2–3 birds' eye chillies, finely sliced

100g fresh coriander leaves, coarsely chopped

100g fresh mint leaves, coarsely chopped

5cm chunk fresh root ginger, shredded

4 tablespoons peanut oil

400g slice rump steak, cut at least 2cm thick (optional)

4 garlic cloves, chopped or shredded

12 spring onions or 1 red onion, sliced

1 tablespoon caster sugar

2 tablespoons dark sesame oil

2 tablespoons fish sauce or light soy sauce

3–4 tablespoons rice vinegar

2 tablespoons roasted sesame seeds (optional)

To prepare/cook Pour boiling water over the dried rice noodles in a colander set in a large heatproof bowl. Leave for 3–4 minutes or until the noodles feel pliable. Drain. Pour cold water over the noodles; leave 3–4 minutes or until cool but do not let them become soft. Drain well and return them to the empty bowl. Add the next 6 ingredients; stir gently to mix. Put 1 tablespoon of the peanut oil into a non-stick frying pan. Heat until very hot; add the steak, if using. Cook for 1–1 1/2 minutes, turning, or until the outside is brown, the inside rare. Cool. Slice the steak into fine, ribbon-like strips. Combine the remaining peanut oil with the remaining ingredients. Shake well, pour over the salad and toss gently. Cover and leave to stand. Take the salad in a snap-top container; wrap the beef and its juices in foil or plastic wrap.

To present Divide the salad between the serving bowls; add strips of rare beef for those who like it, adding some of the juices as well. Serve cool.

Sweet feasts

Ripe hedgerow berries, ice creams at the seaside, rock or nougat from a village confectioner, sticky pastries from a local bakery: these are often some of the simplest, easiest sweet treats of all for portable feasting. But included in this section are some interesting cakes and cookies, some chocolate and fruit desserts, and all the means by which you can keep them looking, as well as tasting, good.

Pashka *page 106*

Mixed Fruits Salad *page 109*

Raspberry Fool *page 113*

Sweet things have probably been loved by mankind ever since wild honey was discovered, aeons ago, and today most of us still regard one or two sweet things at the conclusion of a meal as a right and fitting gesture to round off the savoury tastes.

One classic dessert, for many Europeans, is cheese followed by fresh fruit, and perhaps nuts. This is still a good policy, especially if the fruit is scented and sweet, the cheese at its peak, the nuts mellow.

But sometimes we want more frivolity: something small but interestingly sweet to intrigue our palates and make us feel indulged.

For portable feasting, ready-made cookies, cakes, chocolate, and set desserts, each in its own little pot, are practical ideas.

Some dessert ideas can be made on the spot: crushing berries and sugar, folding them into cream and crunching up meringues to add texture must be one of the most intriguing. This is included here, along with lemon-scented, chocolate-based, nut-enriched sweet things.

Some have a rich dairy basis: pashka is an example, as is Munster cheese with ripe pears. Others are fruit based: my fruit salad is a wondrously eclectic one. Frothy white angel cake is a pleasure because it seems so summery and fresh. Yet it can be made in the depths of winter and served with tea or coffee.

Many of the other sections of this book will give you ideas for creating your own sweet feasts. Pour some lemon cordial from the lemonade recipe (see page 122) over some thick natural yogurt or a bowlful of berries, add a crisp bought biscotti, amaretti, sponge finger or nutty wafer and you've customised your very own dessert.

Make a flaskful of smoothie recipe (page 120) and pour some, chilled, over platefuls of sliced banana, mango, pineapple or melon and you've a vitamin-rich pudding.

Many savoury and sweet feasts can be concluded stylishly by serving a glass of some superb sweet wine or liqueur. These are all great tastes to accompany coffees, teas, tisanes, the natural ending to many fine meals.

Certain sweet feasts happen naturally: wild tangles of brambles or bilberries; wood strawberries; wild cherries; ripe plums from overhanging branches; tiny sweet, sharp apples on a mossy old tree all but forgotten by the passers-by. These can be the best sort of treat: free bounty for us all.

Angel Cake

with Citrus Frosting

Angel cake, or Angel Food Cake, is made without any egg yolks so it is white, fluffy and so ephemeral that it really does deserve its name. Vanilla, almond and citrus flavours are a feature of this indulgent offering with its generous frosting. Transport this special cake carefully, and decorate with green grapes, citrus slices or wild flowers if you like.

Serves 8

To buy/find

Angel Cake:

7 egg whites, at room temperature

pinch of salt

1/2 teaspoon cream of tartar

225g caster sugar

75g plain flour or cake flour, sifted

1 teaspoon almond essence

Frosting:

450g cream cheese

100g icing sugar, sifted

shredded zest of 2 limes and a little juice

1/4–1/2 teaspoon almond essence

To prepare/cook Have ready a large, deep ring-shaped cake tin with removable base (angel-cake tin). (Do not grease or flour it.) Combine the egg whites and salt with the cream of tartar, in a large clean bowl. Using an electric whisk or rotary beater, whisk continuously until the mix stands up in soft peaks. Set aside 50g caster sugar; add the remaining caster sugar, about a heaped tablespoon at a time, continuously whisking. Mix the 50g caster sugar with the sifted flour. Fold half of this mixture into the whisked whites gently and firmly, using broad strokes in a 'figure of eight' shape. Continue with the next half. Stir in the essence and smooth it gently through the cake batter. Smooth this batter into the cake tin. Bake at the centre of an oven preheated to 190°C for 28–30 minutes. Reduce the heat to 140°C and continue to cook for 16–18 minutes. Test the cake: it should feel slightly springy to the touch and be shrinking a little from the edges. Remove from the oven and let it stand for 10 minutes; run a knife around the edges to help loosen the cake. Put a rack on top. Invert both quickly, giving a little tap to loosen the cake. Cool the turned-out cake on a rack. Beat the frosting ingredients together using a minimal amount of juice – it must not become too soft. Frost the cake all over and transport it in a snap-top plastic or metal cake box, setting the cake on the lid and closing it by pushing the base on to it from above. Keep the box this way up.

To present Undo the box on the spot, when you are ready to eat, and decorate as you like.

Note:

If the day is very hot, try to keep the cake cool and fresh. Do not freeze it. Both cake and frosting can, however, be made, and chilled, in their containers, a day in advance.

Pashka

with Fruits

Traditionally these little Russian puddings came as part of a spring celebration: a profusion of dairy products and dried fruits being some of the original features. But make them at any time, any season. Use one large bowl or several small 'timbale' moulds or even small glass tumblers. With the help of a strip of foil, each pudding is easily removed at serving time and the shapes stay perfect.

Serves 8

To buy/find

400g full-fat cream cheese

250g curd cheese, quark or low fat soft cheese

4 tablespoons citrus liqueur e.g. Limoncello or Mandarine, plus extra to decorate

6–8 tablespoons clear honey

75g fresh yellow cake crumbs

1/2 teaspoon orange flower water

2 teaspoons grated orange zest

75g chopped mixed peel

75g flaked almonds

To prepare/make Combine all the ingredients in a large bowl or a food processor. Stir energetically to mix or process, in brief bursts, in the food processor until the mix is uniform in consistency. Taste. Add extra honey if needed. Cut 8 strips of aluminium foil about 12 x 4cm in size. Fold in half lengthwise, twice. Press the strips into 8 small, metal 'timbale' moulds (about 100ml volume) so the strips lie smoothly across the base and up the sides. Leave the excess to use as 'handles'. Spoon in the pashka mixture and press it down well. Chill for several hours or overnight. Transport to the site in the moulds. Invert each pudding, and pull the foil strip downwards, unmoulding each one on to a plate.

To present Pour a pool of liqueur round each tower-shaped pudding.

Mixed Fruits Salad

with Passion Fruit

A luscious, fresh fruit dessert which is vividly scented and colourful. Substitute seasonal fruits for any of those suggested. The essential, however, is the fresh passion fruit. Without these this is just a fruit salad. Remember that passion fruit – in their hard wrinkly shells – will keep for weeks in your refrigerator. Pomegranate molasses is a sharp, sweet, scented Middle Eastern condiment: look for it in ethnic grocers.

Serves 8

To buy/find

12 fresh passion fruit (about 400–650g), washed and halved

1/2 teaspoon orange flower, geranium or rose water

2 tablespoons pomegranate molasses or crème de cassis

500g fresh peaches, white- or yellow-fleshed, pitted and in chunks

4 fresh, ripe figs, green or black, halved lengthwise

4 ripe nectarines or red-fleshed plums, pitted and in chunks

250g cherries, still on the stalk

250g orange- or green-fleshed melon, seeded, in 5cm chunks

juice of 4 minneolas, tangelos, tangerines or satsumas

To prepare/make Scoop the flesh out of half of the passion fruit. Combine the flesh in a blender with the flower water and the pomegranate molasses or cassis. Give 8 or 10 short, sharp blitzes: you want to separate the seeds from the pulp to obtain an intense syrup. Strain the pulp through a non-metal sieve and discard the seeds. Select a beautiful, but portable deep dish or glass jug. Add the syrup, the remaining passion fruit, halved but otherwise intact, the peaches, figs, nectarines, cherries and the melon. Stir. Add the citrus juice. Stir gently.

To present Let people help themselves.

Munster

with Pears

Though unctuous and silky to eat and deceptively mild, the strong aroma of Munster is often enough to deter many a diner. It combines blissfully with ripe pears.

Serves 8

To buy/find

small Munster cheese (a washed-rind cheese from Alsace), about 225g

8 ripe but firm dessert pears

To prepare/make If your Munster is a little underripe, be bold: heat it, still paper-wrapped, in an oven preheated to 230°C for 5 minutes or else use a microwave (700–850 watts) on High for 2 minutes. This acts as an accelerated ripening process. The effect is intense. Take the cheese to the picnic just as it is. It will begin to trickle and run before too long. Leave the stalks on the pears. Using an apple corer, push upwards from the base of each pear almost to the top stem area. Do not sever nor twist. At serving time, push down on the stem area and remove the core.

To present Unwrap the cheese just as you begin to eat. Leave the pears whole. Let guests use knives or fingers to eat their 100% edible pear.

Pecan & Chocolate Brownies

Few people I know can resist a good chocolate brownie, soft, rich and dark. This recipe is one such. Make these brownies in minutes; transport them still warm. They combine well with vanilla ice-cream, cream, fromage frais, pouring custard, berry coulis, fudge sauce or a combination of some of these. But serving them plain or dusted with a little icing sugar often seems sufficient.

Makes 16 pieces

To buy/find

125g butter, cubed, softened

200g plain, bitter chocolate (ideally 70% cocoa solids), broken

150g caster sugar

2 eggs, beaten

1 teaspoon vanilla essence

115g plain flour, sifted

200g pecan nut halves or pieces

icing sugar, for dusting (optional)

To prepare/cook Melt the butter and half of the chocolate in a large heatproof jug or bowl, using a microwave (700–850 watts) on High for 1–1½ minutes or over a steamer. Stir well. Add the sugar, eggs and vanilla and whisk using an electric beater until evenly blended. Add the flour and use a spatula to gently fold it through the mix until it is a thick, rich, dark batter with no floury areas. Do not overmix. Cover the base of a 20cm square baking tin with non-stick paper or teflon fabric. Smooth the batter out into the prepared baking tin. Scatter the nuts and the remaining chocolate pieces over, pushing some well in. Bake in an oven preheated to 180°C for 17–18 minutes. The edges should look firm but the centre barely cooked; the residual heat will continue cooking out of the oven. Allow to cool a little and score into 16 squares.

To present Transport in the baking tin, dusting with icing sugar once cool. Or, if you like, serve with ice-cream or the other suggested accompaniments.

Macadamia, Lime & White Chocolate Cookies

Though these cookies need careful handing when newly cooked, crumbly and still warm, they are easy, homely and have a subtle flavour. Decorate them in whatever idiosyncratic way you like. It may seem odd to use salted nuts, but it helps balance the sweetness of the dough and the richness of the chocolate.

Makes 24–32

To buy/find

300g salted macadamia nuts

250g spreadable butter

125g vanilla sugar

2 teaspoons fresh lime zest, shredded

2 tablespoons freshly squeezed lime juice

300g self-raising flour

150g white chocolate, broken

3 tablespoons single cream

To prepare/cook Toast the macadamia nuts in a preheated oven at 160–170°C for 15–20 minutes or so until they are dry, hot but not browned. Cool them. Hand chop 50g of them coarsely and keep these aside. Using a cook's knife, mezzaluna or a food processor, in brief bursts, chop the remainder to a coarse meal, but do not over-process. Cream the butter and sugar using an electric whisk or rotary beater until pale and light. Stir in the nut 'meal', the zest and juice, then the flour. Mix, then knead in the bowl to compact the dough into a dense, soft ball. Roll it out between two sheets of plastic wrap to about 3mm thickness. Use cutters (hearts, diamonds, circles etc.) to cut out 24–32 shapes, each about 5–7cm diameter. Re-roll any left-over dough and use this for more shapes. Lift the soft dough shapes using a fish slice and slide them off using a palette knife. Set them, about 2cm apart, on 2 large baking trays ideally lined with non-stick paper or fabric. Adjust oven temperature to 150°C and bake for 20–23 minutes or until pale golden, crisp but pliable. Remove the oven trays. Let them stand for 10 minutes then remove the cookies to wire racks to cool. Heat the white chocolate and cream over boiling water or using a microwave (700–850 watts) on High for three 20-second bursts, or until melted. Stir until smooth. Use the melted chocolate and a pastry brush to paint patterns, or part-dip the cookies or drizzle chocolate over them. Push on the reserved chopped macadamia nuts. Cool until cold and set. Store in an airtight container, between layers of greaseproof paper, and serve and eat whenever you like.

Lemon Squares

This recipe is always a favourite. The sharpness and sweetness – the softness and crustiness – provide unusual but intriguing contrasts. The old fashioned charms of this sweet treat ensure its popularity.

Makes 16

To buy/find

Crust:

200g plain flour

135g icing sugar

25g cornflour

175g salted butter, chilled

Topping:

5 eggs, beaten

285g granulated sugar

4 tablespoons plain flour

3 teaspoons lemon zest, grated or shredded (from 2 lemons)

175ml freshly squeezed lemon juice (from 3–4 lemons)

120ml full-fat milk

1/8 teaspoon salt

extra icing-sugar, for dusting (optional)

To prepare/cook Preheat the oven to 180°C and set a rack in the middle. Butter a 22.5 x 20.5cm baking tin or sponge roll tin: it should have sides at least 1.5cm deep. Double-line the baking tin with foil, overhanging at each end, and smooth it flat. To make the crust, put the flour, icing sugar, cornflour and butter into a food processor. Process for 8 seconds then pulse minimally, in repeated bursts, until the butter is evenly distributed and the mix looks yellow and gritty in texture. Scatter this all over the foil. Press into the baking tin making it rise up slightly at the edges. Chill for 30 minutes. Bake for 25–28 minutes or until pale and golden. Reduce oven temperature to 170°C. Combine the 7 topping ingredients and whisk until blended. Pour on to the crust. Bake for 20 minutes or until the topping is soft and custard-like, but set. Remove and cool in the tin on a wire rack for at least 30 minutes. Use a pizza cutter or knife to mark into 16 cookies. Do not remove from the tin. Fold over the excess foil to cover. Wrap again in plastic wrap. Take the icing sugar separately.

To present Pull up the foil to remove the cookies in one large block from their tin. Dust with icing sugar if you like and serve. Use with tea and coffee, as a sweet snack or light dessert.

Raspberry Fool

with Meringues

This is an ingenious recipe. The 'impossible' meringue idea, from my sister Alison, works brilliantly and makes quick, foolproof meringues: 80–100 or so. These are small, crisp and can be stored, in airtight jars, for months. But if you'd prefer to use purchased meringues this too is an option. The actual dessert is assembled pretty much on the spot: its crunch, softness, sweetness and sharpness is a pleasant paradox.

Serves 8

To buy/find

'Impossible' meringues:

325g caster sugar

2 egg whites

1 teaspoon vanilla essence

1 teaspoon malt vinegar

60ml boiling water

Note: Makes 80–100 tiny meringues. Substitution: 200g bought meringues

Berry fool:

350g fresh raspberries

50g icing sugar, plus extra for dusting

450ml double cream, whipped or 600ml extra-thick, double cream

To prepare/cook Combine the 5 meringue ingredients, in order, in a heatproof bowl standing in 2.5cm of near-boiling water. Using an electric whisk or rotary beater, whisk continuously until the unpromising-looking mix forms a dense, glossy, stiff meringue which will keep its shape. Remove the bowl from the water. Set some wetted non-stick paper on 2 large oven trays. Wet the surface of these again. Put the meringue into a piping-bag with a 1cm star nozzle. Pipe 80–100 small, neat meringues. Bake at 130–140°C for 1–1¼ hours or until crisp. Take as many as you want to the picnic along with the berries, sugar and cream, in insulated containers. Take a bowl along to the site in which to mash everything together.

To present Mash the berries and sugar roughly with a fork and trickle this purée into the cream, adding whole or smashed meringues at will. Dust with a little icing sugar and serve in glasses, cups or platefuls.

Chocolate Cream Pots

These are lush, luxurious, indulgent desserts to finish off a perfect meal.

Serves 8

To buy/find

2 tablespoons double cream

200g bitter chocolate, broken into bits

50g icing sugar

2 teaspoons ground cinnamon

4 tablespoons Amaretto di Saronno or Cointreau liqueur

400g mascarpone

1 box crisp wafers or chocolate matchsticks, to serve

To prepare/cook Put the cream and the chocolate bits into a large heatproof bowl or jug and microwave (700–850 watts) on High for 2–2½ minutes, stirring occasionally, until it is melted. Alternatively, set it in a heatproof bowl or jug over a pan of boiling water and stir until melted. Sift the icing sugar and cinnamon together and stir into the chocolate mixture, then stir in the liqueur. Mix until creamy. Fold in the mascarpone to obtain a marbled effect. Spoon, pipe or smooth the chocolate cream into 8 small china or glass pots to be taken to the picnic. Do not overfill them. Firm them up by placing them in the freezer for 20 minutes, or chill for several hours or overnight. Pack the pots into a larger box with a lid, or wrap them securely in foil into one large packet. Unwrap at serving time.

To present Put a little stack of fine wafers such as *crêpes à dentelles* or chocolate matchsticks beside each dessert.

Drinks

Tall, frosted tumblers, cubes of ice clinking and the gush of juice, water or wine into a glass: these are extremely welcome signs at any convivial meal. On the other hand, it may be a hot, spicy, sweet coffee you yearn for, a fruit-boosted smoothie to soothe your thirst. Good drinks spell real pleasure and can complement any portable feast in an uniquely satisfying way. The ideas included here are no exception.

Refreshing, appropriate and imaginatively chosen drinks can enhance a meal in an enjoyable way. Even a well selected bottle of spring water can flatter the food: in fact most people would consider this an absolute essential. Some beer bottles in a wicker basket cooling in a mountain stream; a battered saucepan of aromatised tea or coffee set in the embers of a dying fire to heat – these are delightful, easy ideas.

But for the more usual occasions the obvious answer is to use insulated containers: vacuum flasks or jugs for hot or iced drinks, portable 'chiller-bins' which can be filled with ice; pre-frozen 'sleeves' to slip around your bottle of water, wine, juice or cordial. Another idea is to create a special herb-decorated ice jacket around a bottle of frozen vodka and use this as a portable freezer in its own right.

Tea, coffee and herb tisanes are easy drink solutions but elderflower tea, tea with rum, mint, or tea infused by the sun using just a jug of water are all included here. Quality tea, sold loose, is better than tea bags but this means you'll need a square of muslin and a piece of string to tie up the tea, or a metal, perforated, clip-closed tea infuser. It is also possible to buy a heatproof glass 'tea-press' (like a teapot) with a central insert for the leaves. But a plunger-type coffee pot works for tea and for coffee: so does a battered old metal teapot: be inventive. A big sieve will do, if all else fails . . .

Vanilla coffee, an indulgent treat, is another idea. Serve it in tiny unbreakable cups, in mugs or in toughened glasses or tumblers.

Many people who enjoyed their grandmother's recipes for lemonade, limeade and ginger beer as children, have forgotten how to make them. I include recipes for these here. The cocktails included are guaranteed to make any feast into a real celebration: from the classic martini (for grown-ups) to mint julep; from Silver Gin Fizz to Virgine Maria, a cocktail with no alcohol at all.

The joy is that cocktails and mixed drinks are so very diverse. They can be simple or complex; citrussy or nutty; layered or blended; mild or potent; floral or herbal; decorative or plain; alcohol-boosted or absolutely alcohol-free.

For cocktails, you'll need a jug and shaker, or both, the glasses, a corkscrew, a bottle opener, a small sharp knife, a long-handled spoon, a drinks strainer which ideally fits over a pouring lip, a citrus squeezer (the wand type is useful), lots of ice, and the cocktail raw materials, ideally chilled. A 'measure' is usually made of metal and holds 25ml volume. Use a small shot glass as an alternative, or 2 level measuring tablespoons (30ml) which is slightly larger but conveniently approximate. Otherwise take along a small toughened glass measuring jug.

Almost any appropriately sized glass will do, especially if it is made of toughened glass. Don't forget that waxed paper cups, plastic tumblers; porcelain, metal and even bamboo containers can all be useful and appealing as drinks containers. Remember to offer lots of still and sparkling water for all who want it: in the end this is the most magnificent drink of all.

Frozen vodka

To make this decorative ice jacket, take a large empty plastic bottle and cut off the top just below the shoulders. Place the vodka bottle centrally in the plastic sleeve, and fill the cylinder with water. Push bay sprigs, pretty leaves or flowers, colourful berries or lemon slices into the water around the vodka bottle and place the whole – upright – in a freezer for at least 24 hours. Take it to your picnic complete. The outer plastic will slide off when slightly warmed – either after the travelling time, or after a little warm hand pressure. The vodka will pour thickly. Enjoy its opulent cold texture and taste!

Elderflower Tea

These days, ready-made elderflower syrup is available from delis, good grocers and even some supermarkets. Though sweet, it is flowery and fresh. Use it along with a delicate China tea and, if real elderflower is blooming, add some heads of flowers too.

Serves 8

To buy/find

1 litre boiling water

10g China tea, e.g. jasmine

2 tablespoons elderflower syrup or cordial

2 fresh elderflower heads, if in season

To prepare/make Use a heatproof glass jug, vacuum flask, whatever pleases you and suits the occasion. Pour the water over the tea, tied up in muslin or in a tea infuser, and leave to infuse for 5 minutes. Remove the tea 'bag' or infuser and pour in the syrup or cordial.

To present Push the flowerheads (rinsed in spring water) into the tea at serving time. Serve in small cups, goblets or tumblers.

Note:

If made double strength (using only 500ml of boiling water) and poured over 500ml of ice cubes, this can become a chilled drink, instead of a hot one.

Scented Tea

with Rum

Tea made with added aromatics can be very alluring. Select either China, Indian or another exotic tea from Sri Lanka or Nepal. Vary the additions according to the type of tea you started off with.

Serves 4–6

To buy/find

1 litre boiling water

1 cinnamon stick, crushed

4 cloves

6 green cardamom pods, crushed

7.5cm strip of orange zest or 2.5cm piece of fresh root ginger, bruised

15g tea leaves

150ml dark rum, ideally Stroh type

1 orange, pith removed, sliced into rounds

To prepare/make Pour the boiling water over the cinnamon, cloves, cardamom pods, bring back to the boil, cover, reduce heat to simmering. Simmer for 3–4 minutes. Put the zest and tea, in a tie of muslin with a string attached, or in a tea infuser, into a vacuum flask. Pour in the boiling spiced liquid, including all spices. Stopper the flask. Infuse for 5 minutes then remove the tea and zest. If taking to a picnic, take along another flask of plain boiling water, and the rum in a separate bottle.

To present Pour the tea, and add slices of orange and a dash of rum to each serving of the hot spiced tea.

Mint Tea

Tunisian tea houses taught me how refreshing this hot, sweet tea can be. Don't stint on the fresh mint: it is crucial to its success.

Serves 8

To buy/find

1 litre boiling water

15g green (unfermented) tea

150g bunch fresh mint, ideally spearmint, lower stems discarded

16–24 sugar lumps or 8 tablespoons caster sugar

sliced lemon or lime, to decorate

To prepare/make Pour the boiling water over the tea, tied up in muslin or in a tea infuser, in a jug or vacuum flask, adding half of the mint. Crush and press the mint then seal and leave to infuse.

To present Add sugar to each cup, glass or goblet, and a share of the remaining mint. Crush the mint and pour the hot tea over. Decorate with sliced lemon or lime.

Sun Tea

At its most homely, this can be made in a jug of water, sitting in a sunny spot with some fragrant tea bags suspended in it. Once infused, the tea bags are removed. This is the basis of sun tea. Boost it with a little lemon cordial, some sliced lemon, lime or orange. Add a few sprigs of fresh mint, lovage or bergamot. Ice and a top-up of sparkling water, ginger ale or tonic improves it too. This is a thirst-quencher, alcohol-free, of simplicity and merit.

Serves 8

To buy/find

6 good quality tea bags or 15g loose tea (tied in muslin or in a tea infuser) e.g. China or Indian, mixed red fruits or Japanese green tea

1 litre spring water, tap water or filtered water, at room temperature

ice cubes

handful of fresh mint, lovage, bergamot or lemon balm leaves

2–3 tablespoons lemonade, undiluted (see page 122)

1 lemon, 2 limes or 1 orange, sliced

iced sparkling water, ginger ale, tonic or even lemonade, to top up

To prepare/make Leave the tea to infuse in the non-chilled water. This may take 30 minutes or 2 hours depending on the temperature, the type of tea and the situation. Stir occasionally. Strain. Pour into a flask, bottle or jar. Take along the remaining items: ice, fresh herbs, lemonade, citrus fruits, and the top-up liquid of your choice.

To present On site, crush the herbs and sliced citrus in a big glass jug with the ice. Pour the sun tea over. Add the top-up liquid to taste. Drink cold.

Coffee

with Calvados

'Calva' with or in coffee is a delightful French idea. Add sugar – or not – to this fragrant coffee, depending on your taste buds.

Serves 8

To buy/find

520ml freshly made, hot coffee

8 sugar lumps (optional)

120ml Calvados, apple brandy or apple jack

To make/present Transport the hot coffee in a vacuum jug or flask. Combine a share of hot coffee, some sugar, if liked, and some of Calvados in each *demitasse* coffee cup. Stir, sip and enjoy. Alternatively, serve the coffee as is, taking along 8 tiny shot glasses. Serve a shot of Calvados per person in each glass, as an additional pleasure.

Vanilla Coffee

In Mexico, Café de Olla, an after-dinner drink, is sometimes served in big countrified earthenware pitchers. Adapt this idea for your own celebrations. It is festive and fun.

Serves 8

To buy/find

4 vanilla pods, sliced almost into halves, lengthwise

1 litre boiling water

4 teaspoons cloves, bruised

4 teaspoons allspice berries

200g dark muscovado sugar

5cm strip orange zest, bruised

2 litres freshly made *cafétière* coffee, e.g. Brazilian

To prepare/make Scrape out the seeds from the vanilla pods. In a saucepan, heat together the water, vanilla seeds, cloves, allspice and muscovado sugar for 5 minutes, stirring. Add the orange zest, crushing it down well. Turn off the heat. Let it infuse 2 minutes. Remove the orange zest, and take this spicy syrup, in a stoppered, heatproof vacuum flask, or in a heatproof jug which can be set directly on the barbecue, to the *parilla*.

To present Reheat the syrup over the fire if necessary. Pour out some hot coffee into cups, mugs or glasses. Add a top-up of hot syrup. Pass the completed vanilla coffee around to your friends.

Note:

You could add half a cinnamon stick per person, too, if you like.

Smoothies, Crushes & Variations

Although these can now often be purchased, ready-made, in supermarkets or made while you wait at a juice bar, your own customised combinations are freshest and best. Vary these according to the fruits available. To simplify the process use a half-cup measure or even a wine glass as your volume measure (about 125ml or so). Keep the units constant. But relax: this is a free and easy concept. You'll also need a large and sturdy blender which is not damaged by ice. If using a juicer, juice the solids and use a blender to combine these with the rest if banana is used, or whisk or shake until cold and blended.

Each drink serves 4

Pineapple-Honey-Citrus Smoothie

To buy/find

2 parts natural yogurt, ideally live

2 parts cubed fresh pineapple

2 parts freshly squeezed orange or grapefruit juice

1/2 part clear honey

1 part ice cubes

To prepare/make Combine the first 4 ingredients in a blender. Blend. Add the ice and blend again until the ice is no longer visible and the drink is a thickish liquid. Add a little water if liked, to thin it slightly.

To present If made ahead, store it in a vacuum flask but take extra ice and shake the smoothie well to chill it again before serving, or pour it over the ice in the glasses or containers. Serve with thick straws.

Variations

Raspberry-Pineapple Smoothie

To prepare/make Make as before adding 2 parts fresh or thawed raspberries and use orange, not grapefruit juice. Blend these first 5 ingredients and then the ice.

Plum, Banana and Blackberry Smoothie

2 parts natural yogurt, ideally live

1 part fresh or thawed blackberries

1 part cubed, red-fleshed plums

1 part chopped banana

2 parts freshly squeezed blood orange or orange juice

1/2 part clear honey

1 part ice cubes

To prepare/make Make as before, blending the first 6 ingredients, then the ice cubes.

Mango, Raspberry and Orange Crush

2 parts cubed fresh mango

1 part chopped banana

1/4 part fresh or thawed raspberries

2 parts freshly squeezed orange juice

1 part ice cubes

To prepare/make Make as before, blending the first 4 ingredients, then the ice cubes.

Home-Made

Ginger Beer Fizz

Sadly this old favourite is not often made at home these days. This drink is easy, inexpensive and utterly refreshing. Use plastic, not glass bottles, and the risk of exploding bottles is avoided. Go for screw-tops. This is a traditional drink well worth celebrating. You'll need a large, clean plastic bucket and eight 1-litre plastic bottles.

Makes 8 litres

To buy/find

2 teaspoons dried yeast granules

900g granulated sugar

2 tablespoons ground ginger

1 tablespoon lemonade, undiluted (see right) or 1/2 teaspoon lemon oil

2 teaspoons tartaric acid

950ml hot water

5 litres cold water

To serve: Ice, sliced lemon; drinking straws (optional)

To prepare/make Stir the yeast granules with about 1/4 cup (60ml) of warm water and 1 teaspoon of the sugar. Put the remaining sugar, the ginger, cordial or lemon oil and tartaric acid into a clean plastic bucket. Stir in the hot water until the sugar is dissolved. Add the cold water. Stir in the yeast mix, with a whisk, until it is evenly distributed. Using a funnel, pour the ginger beer into 8 clean, flexible plastic bottles. Pour boiling water over the screw tops, and drain them. Pinch the shoulders at the top of the bottle to allow space for expansion then screw on the tops. Leave the bottles at normal room temperature for at least 4–6 days. During this time the pressure will increase: to start with the bottles have give; later tightness means that fizz and pressure are developing. Test one bottle; when the beer tastes slightly fizzy, refrigerate them all.

To present Drink chilled. Try to avoid shaking the bottles. Serve over ice with lemon and drinking straws.

Home-Made

Lemonade & Soda

The easiest method for this is the French *citron pressé* idea: slices of lemon and some squeezed juice, sugar and some sparkling mineral water. But my lemon cordial is brilliantly convenient too: use it with sparkling water, lager, in cocktails, in sun tea, over sorbets and ices as well as with plain water. The citric acid sharpens the taste and Epsom salts acts as a harmless preservative: buy these from chemist's shops or specialist grocers.

Serves 6–8

To buy/find

400ml water

400g sugar

zest, in fine shreds, and juice of 8 lemons

3 teaspoons citric acid

1/2 teaspoon Epsom salts (magnesium sulphate)

zest of 1 orange, in fine shreds

3 litres sparkling water, to dilute

ice, to serve

drinking straws (optional)

To prepare/make Boil the water with the sugar to make a hot syrup. Add the lemon juice and stir well; add the citric acid and Epsom salts. Add the lemon and orange zests, stir well and remove from the heat. Allow to stand for 2 minutes. Strain well to remove the zest shreds. The colour should be a bright golden yellow. Cool the syrup over ice. Pour it into a bottle, a vacuum flask or stoppered jug.

To present Take iced sparkling water, spring water or soda to dilute it. Take, too, some ice cubes in an insulated container or buy some en route. Dilute about 1 part cordial to 3–4 parts sparkling water and serve with some ice cubes, and straws if you like.

Note:

Fresh herbs such as lovage, fresh mint, lemon balm or even crushed kaffir lime leaves may also be added as a decoration. So can slices or wedges of any citrus fruit of of your choice.

Home-Made

Limeade

This, too, uses the *citron pressé* concept: adding extra lime zest boosts flavours, too, as does the vanilla-scented sugar. Add bitters or a little alcohol, if you like.

Serves 4

To buy/find

5 fresh limes, one with zest removed in 4 long strips

4 tablespoons vanilla or caster sugar

iced soda water, to top up

ice cubes or crushed ice, to top up

To prepare/make 'Muddle' or mash up one strip of lime in each of the bases of 4 tall glasses with its share of sugar. Squeeze all the limes. Divide this juice between the glasses. Stir them again until the sugar is dissolved. Heap in some ice: half-fill each glass. Top up with soda water. Stir. Serve with drinking straws.

Variations

Bitter Limeade Shake in some Peychaud bitters, Angostura bitters or orange bitters. Stir.

Chilli Limeade In India this is sometimes called *nimbu pani*. Omit the sugar. Add a whole fresh chilli to each glass, pushed on to a satay or cocktail stick, and a sprinkle of salt in place of the sugar.

Kaffir Limeade Add 1 fresh kaffir lime leaf (washed and crushed) to each drink at the end of mixing. Stir. (Substitute lemon-scented verbena as an alternative.)

Virgine Maria

This is a Bloody Mary without alcohol but with one or two other interesting ingredients and lots of ice to make it more refreshing. Give it either an Asian or a Mexican twist according to your mood. Take it along already mixed. Shake again with ice, on site. Garnish and serve.

Serves 4

To buy/find

2 fresh limes

2 fresh lemons

600ml tomato juice, 'clamato' juice or mixed tomato-vegetable juice

4 teaspoons Worcestershire sauce

2 teaspoons *wasabi* paste or 1/2 teaspoon smoked hot paprika

2 teaspoons light soy sauce or 1 teaspoon of sea salt

16 ice cubes

4 sticks fresh celery with leaves

To make/present

Remove long loopy curls of zest from the limes and lemons and reserve. Squeeze the limes and lemons. Combine the tomato juice, lime and lemon juice, Worcestershire sauce, *wasabi* or paprika, and soy sauce or salt in a blender, shaker or jug. Blend, shake or stir. Pour into 4 long slim glasses. Add ice cubes to each glass, a stick of celery to stir and curls of zest.

Silver Gin Fizz

This is a shaken cocktail topped up with soda. Either mix the ingredients in a large shaker, add ice at the last minute and shake, or else take all the ingredients separately and make the drink on site. Have lowball or medium-long glasses for this.

Serves 8

To buy/find

16 ice cubes

2 tablespoons sugar syrup (*sirop de gomme*) or 2 tablespoons caster sugar

200ml freshly squeezed lemon juice

600ml dry gin

4 fresh egg whites

chilled soda water, to top up

To make/present

Combine the first 5 ingredients in a large shaker or even a screw-top jar. Shake until frothy. Strain into six lowball glasses or short tumblers. Top up with chilled soda and serve.

Variations

Outback Replace the fresh lemon with 150ml of dry French vermouth.

Morning Glory Fizz This has a teaspoon of Pernod added and the top-up is ginger ale, not soda.

Note:

For sugar syrup, boil 250ml water and 250g caster sugar until the sugar dissolves.

Mint Julep

For this drink you need sugar, ice, bourbon and good, fresh mint in decent quantities. To 'muddle' two ingredients means to gently mash and crush them using a long-handled spoon to extract the maximum flavour and aroma. Any long-handled, blunt implement will do, even a knife handle.

Serves 4

To buy/find

about 16 large, fresh mint sprigs

4 teaspoons caster sugar

300ml crushed ice

300ml bourbon (rye whiskey)

To prepare/make Make these directly in the 4 long glasses or 4 silver mugs. Put 3 sprigs of mint into the base of each glass. Add the sugar. Muddle or mash these two well together to extract the flavours. Stir in some crushed ice into each glass. Muddle again. Pour in the bourbon. Stir. Top up with extra crushed ice. Add the remaining mint sprig to the glasses and serve.

Variations

Mint-Lime Julep Add a thick wedge of lime to the mint-sugar mix. Continue as above.

Bitter Mint-Lime Julep To either of the drinks mentioned above add 2 shakes of Peychaud's or Angostura bitters to each glass. Do not stir. Leave as a 'blush'. Drink through straws.

Pisco Julep Substitute Pisco (Peruvian grape brandy) for the bourbon.

Applejack Julep Use applejack, Calvados or apple brandy in place of the bourbon.

Grown-up Martini

Some grown-up drinkers, serious martini *aficionados*, merely pass the vermouth bottle, still closed, over the top of the glass adding not a drop. Others rinse out the glass with it. Here is a recipe, rather stronger than usual, which is stirred, not shaken.

Serves 8

To buy/find

360ml London dry gin

60ml dry vermouth

12–16 ice cubes

8 green olives (optional)

8 x 7.5cm strips of lemon zest (optional)

To prepare/make Have the 8 glasses ready chilled; put them in the freezer for at least an hour or pack in an insulated bag full of ice for outdoor feasts. Stir the gin and the vermouth together in a large jug over the ice cubes. Into each glass pour a share of the martini. Drop in an olive or a lemon twist. Alternatively twist the lemon above each drink or rub the zest around the glass rim.

Variations

Gin & It Substitute dry red vermouth for the dry vermouth, but use equal quantities of gin and vermouth.

Vodkatini Substitute Stolichnaya (Russian type) vodka for the gin. Reduce the dry vermouth to 40ml and omit the olives and lemon.

Margaritas by the Jugful

Best made and served by the jugful, this Mexican creation is one of the world's most successful and celebratory of cocktails. More ice means more dilution; crushed ice will give a 'frozen margarita' – like a slush. Less ice means more pure intensity. Judge for yourself which style you prefer, but drunk *al fresco* it's usually easiest to shake the cocktail up with ice cubes and serve it simply. The salt rim is an essential. Serve with salted almonds (see page 20) or macadamia nuts.

Serves 8

To buy/find

350ml gold or white tequila

250ml Cointreau or Grand Marnier

350ml freshly squeezed lime juice

fine sea salt, to decorate

8 lime wedges (optional)

500ml ice cubes or crushed ice

To prepare\make Pour the tequila, liqueur and the lime juice into a large glass or earthenware jug, a generous sized shaker or a flask. Seal. Shake vigorously.

To present Put the salt into a shallow saucer. Rub a lime wedge around each glass rim. Invert each glass in the salt to crust it. Shake off the excess. Drop these lime wedges into the glasses. Stir or shake the margarita up with the measured volume of ice cubes until very cold. If using crushed ice, process in a blender. Pour the cocktail into the jug; pour out into prepared glasses.

Cubanaita Cocktail

A nutty, non-alcoholic, coffee-scented, refreshing cocktail or digestif.

Serves 4

To buy/find

60ml hazelnut syrup

60ml cinnamon syrup

240ml decaffeinated coffee, chilled

8 ice cubes

chilled cola, to top up

8 lime slices or wedges

To make/present Combine the first 4 ingredients in a shaker or jug. Shake or stir well. Pour into four tall Collins glasses. Top each drink up with the cola. Add the lime slices and serve.

Index

Acknowledgements

The publisher wishes to thank Rhona Nuttall and Kathryn Dighton at Muji for all the items they loaned for photography. Muji's containers are superbly practical, they withstand wear and tear and – above all – are aesthetically beautiful as well as functional. To Earth Tones, many thanks for all the divine rugs and throws that were supplied which even kept the crew warm on a few gale-force days.

Also we would like to thank John Lewis Partnership, YHA Adventure Shops and Habitat for their help.

Recommended stores where you can buy cooking equipment and other camping gear:

Blacks

53–54 Rathbone Place
London W1P 1AB
Tel: 020 7636 6645
Branches throughout the UK

YHA Adventure Shops

14 Southampton Street
London WC2 7HY
Tel: 020 7836 8541
Branches throughout the UK

For accessories such as plates, napkins and containers:

The Conran Shop

Michelin House
81 Fulham Road
London SW3 6RD
Tel: 020 7589 7401

Habitat

Branches throughout the UK
Tel: 0845 601 0740

Ikea

2 Drury Way
North Circular Road
London NW10 0TH
Tel: 020 8208 5600
Branches throughout the UK

John Lewis Partnership

Oxford Street
London W1A 1EX
Tel: 020 7629 7711
Branches throughout the UK

Muji

6–17 Tottenham Court Road
London W1P 9DP
and branches
Tel: for stockists 020 8323 2208
www.muji.co.jp

For rugs and other decorative items:

Designers Guild

267 Kings Road
London SW3 5EN
Tel: 020 7351 5775
www.designersguild.com

Earth Tones

36 Trent Avenue
London W5 4TL
Tel: 020 7221 9300
www.earthtones.co.uk

Supermarkets during the summer often stock very good items for your essential kit.

Author's acknowledgements

Thanks to Bethany Heald, assistant food stylist, recipe tester and editorial assistant, and to Christine Boodle of Better Read Limited for her word-processing skills. The following food and wine suppliers and specialist shops have helped immeasurably in the evolution of this book:

Chalmers and Gray, Fishmongers, of Notting Hill Gate, London W11

R. Garcia and Sons, Spanish Delicatessen, of Portobello Road, London W11

Jeroboams Cheese and Wine, of Holland Park Avenue, London W11

David Lidgate of C. Lidgate, Butchers and Charcutiers, of Holland Park Avenue, London W11

Speck, Italian Delicatessen, of Portland Road, Holland Park, London W11

Michanicou Brothers, Greengrocers, of Clarendon Road, London W11

Mr Christian's Delicatessen, of Elgin Crescent, Notting Hill, London W11

Kingsland, The Edwardian Butchers, of Portobello Road, London W11

Portobello Road stallholders and shopkeepers, of London W11, whose vivacity is a constant inspiration.